Alexander Wilmot

**The Story of the Expansion of Southern Africa**

Alexander Wilmot

**The Story of the Expansion of Southern Africa**

ISBN/EAN: 9783741186851

Manufactured in Europe, USA, Canada, Australia, Japa

Cover: Foto ©ninafisch / pixelio.de

Manufactured and distributed by brebook publishing software (www.brebook.com)

Alexander Wilmot

**The Story of the Expansion of Southern Africa**

# [TORY]
## THE
# Southern [...]

BY
A. WILMO[T]
*Council of the C[...]*

London
T. FISHER UNWIN
PATERNOSTER SQUARE
MDCCCXCIV

# PREFACE

THE history of South Africa is full of adventure and romance. Something new of great interest has been constantly discovered, until this portion of the world stands before us as a land of diamonds and of gold, where the oldest auriferous workings of the world have become the newest 'diggings.' The nature, character and conduct of its native races are well worth study, while a narrative of the events during the Dutch rule of the sixteenth and seventeenth centuries unfolds interesting details. From the romance of the Portuguese contemporaries of Columbus, who first doubled the Cape of Storms, to the romance of the daring pioneers of the British Chartered Company, who conquered an empire, there have been events as variable, as remarkable, and as well worthy of study, as those which have occurred in almost any other country of the world. It is a mistake to look upon South African history as full of the details of colonial life which are only interesting to colonists. The contrary is the case. An attempt is now made to tell, in a brief but readable form, the story of the expansion of a country in which one of the greatest and richest empires of the southern seas is now in course of being built up. It is impossible to study thoroughly recent events in one part of South Africa, or developments in any portion of the congerie of states and colonies into which its vast territories are divided, without understanding the subject of its history from the earliest times. There are links which bind in one chain all the periods of the narrative. South Africa should never be studied piecemeal when we are considering its past history or its future career; and it is hoped that this work, by one who has lived in the country of which he writes — when many events to which he refers were occurring — may be acceptable as a contribution to a study which should now engage the attention of every citizen of the Empire who desires to appreciate its opportunities and understand its position.

# CONTENTS

INTRODUCTORY NOTE, . . . . . . . page xiii

### CHAPTER I.
Early History—The Hottentots, Bushmen and Kafirs — Customs, Manners and Characteristics, . . . . . . 1

### CHAPTER II.
Early Portuguese Discovery—Diaz and Da Gama—Dutch and English visit the Cape—The Dutch East India Company forms a Settlement—Van Riebeek the First 'Commander,' . . 18

### CHAPTER III.
Events under Dutch East India Company Rule—The History of a Narrow Monopoly—Arrival of Huguenot Emigrants—The Rule of the Van der Stells—Shipwrecks—Capture of French Ships in Table Bay—War with the Hottentots and Bushmen, . 36

### CHAPTER IV.
The Baron Von Plettenberg—Local Discontent—Naval Engagement between English and French Fleets—The Heroism of Waltemade—The Loss of the *Grosvenor*—Expansion of the Colony—Establishment of New Divisions—State of the Colony—Arrival of Commissioners of Inquiry—War between the French Republic and the Netherlands—The Prince of Orange requests the Colony to submit to Great Britain—Arrival of the British Fleet—Miserable and Discontented State of the People—Surrender of the Colony to the British Crown, . . . . 60

## CHAPTER V.

The New Government under Great Britain—Discontent and Rebellion—Missionary Enterprise—Kafir War—The Cape of Good Hope reverts to the Batavian Republic under the Treaty of Amiens—New Government incomparably better than that of a Dutch East India Company—Cape re-captured by Sir David Baird—The Battle of Blaauwberg—Rule of the British Government—The Earl of Caledon—Hottentot Missionary Difficulties—Another Kafir War—Murder of Landrost Stockenstroom,   - page 80

## CHAPTER VI.

Sir John Cradock—Kafir War and Battle of Grahamstown—The Rebellion and Trial of Bezuidenhout—Grievances of Dutch Colonists—The Settlers of 1820—The Poet Pringle and Liberty of the Press—Inflated Currency and Government Expenditure—Colonel Smith—Another Kafir War—Death of Hintza—Slave Emancipation—Sir George Napier—The War of the Axe—The Emigrant Boers—Christmas Day, 1850—Another Kafir War—Sir George Cathcart—Expansion of the Colony—Representative Institutions,   .   .   .   .   .   .   .   .   103

## CHAPTER VII.

Brief Sketch of Natal History—The Voortrekkers—The Zulus—The Orange River Sovereignty, -   .   .   .   .   .   125

## CHAPTER VIII.

Sir George Grey—The Kafirs checkmated—Sir Philip Wodehouse—Discovery of Diamonds—The South African Republic—President Burgers—Sir Bartle Frere—Kafir War—Difficulties with Cetywayo—The Zulu War—Isandhlwana—Rorke's Drift—Ulundi—Blunders—Annexation of the Transvaal—War with the Boers—Sir George Colley and Majuba Hill—The Land of Goshen—Expansion,   .   .   .   .   .   145

## CHAPTER IX.

Natal again—Representative Institutions, Populations, etc.—The Orange Free State—Brief Sketch of History—Griqualand West as a Separate Crown Colony—Incorporation with the Cape Colony—Cape Events—Germany in Damaraland—The Matabele Nation—Chaka and Lo Bengula,  -  -  -  -  -  page 169

## CHAPTER X.

The Key to Native Politics—Religion—Lo Bengula—The Great Northern Gold Fields—Zimbabye—Monomotapa and Ancient Gold Diggings—The Chartered Company's Pioneers' March—Mashonaland—Difficulties with the Portuguese,  -  -  190

## CHAPTER XI.

Gazaland—Progress of Events in Mashonaland—Nature and Character of the Country—The Matabele persecute and hunt down the Mashonas—Chartered Company Interferes—War with Lo Bengula—Defeat of the Zulu Forces—Death of the King—Conclusion,  -  -  -  -  -  -  -  -  208

## APPENDIX A.

Charter of the British South Africa Company—Order in Council,  239

## APPENDIX B.

An Agreement between Her Majesty's Government and the British South Africa Company relative to Matabeleland and Mashonaland, dated 23d May 1894—Despatch from the Marquis of Ripon,  -  -  -  -  -  -  -  -  271

# INTRODUCTORY NOTE

A VERY brief description or bird's-eye view of the country whose history is essayed seems desirable, the more so as much more attention has been generally paid in England to the study of the geography of ancient Greece and Rome than to that of colonies which are the principal props of British commerce, as well as new fields for the energies of a redundant population.

South Africa extends from Cape Agulhas to the Zambesi, and British Central Africa, under the sway of the British Africa Company, extends far northward even of that river to the neighbourhood of the Great Lakes. This territory far exceeds that of any empire or kingdom. Indeed, the country from the Cape to the Zambesi alone embraces an approximate area of one and a quarter million square miles, and thus is larger than British India, but the total population certainly does not exceed 6,000,000, and out of these only 670,000 are of European extraction.

The Cape Colony is the most southern and most populous portion, and to the northward of it are the Orange Free State, the South African (Transvaal) Republic, Natal, Zululand, Basutoland, British Bechuanaland, the Protectorate of Bechuanaland, Pondoland (now annexed to the Cape Colony), Swaziland, almost on the point of being swallowed up by the South African Republic; and then there are the native states of Amatongoland, Matabeleland, and Ngamiland. The Portuguese possessions on the east coast stretch from Delagoa Bay to Mozambique, and on the west coast, north of the Orange River, are the territories of Great Namaqualand and Damaraland, part of which is under a German Protectorate. Above all, are the great territories administered by the British Africa Company north and south of the Zambesi. The latter, including Mashonaland and a portion of Matabeleland, styled 'Rhodesia.'

One of the most beautiful and attractive parts of South Africa is the first to greet the eyes of the traveller who lands in Capetown, under the shadow of Table Mountain. He finds the metropolis of the colony like a homely picture in a magnificent gilt frame. The charming suburbs can be seen by a drive of twenty miles over the Victoria Road, round a large portion of the peninsula, along slopes washed by the ocean and overhung by mountains, through fertile valleys, smiling vineyards and woody gorges, until, passing through miles of forest, gardens and villas, the old Dutch castle is reached, and we are once more again in a town, founded so far back as 1652, which now comprises 50,000 people, 12,000 of whom are Malays.

Going inland by rail, we soon reach the wine districts *par excellence* of the Cape Colony. Stellenbosch, with its Dutch theological seminary, is embowered in trees. The wine stores, factories and houses of Paarl stretch for several miles through beautiful cultivated country, filled with orange and lemon groves, peach gardens and vineyards, variegated with rows of oak, pine and other trees. Behind a neighbouring mountain range is the Tulbagh and Worcester valley, where the rock scenery is grand, and many fruitful valleys repay the cultivator. If the railway be left at Ceres Road, and the traveller proceed through

Mitchell's Pass, he finds a favourite health resort, Ceres, which is 2000 feet above sea level. Ascending still further, the heights of the Cold Bokkeveld are reached, where the mountains attain their highest point (6840 feet) in the lofty Winterhoek peak. On one side the streams flow to the Oliphants River, which empties itself into the Atlantic, and on the other side flows the Breede River, which flows into the Indian Ocean, after winding through the districts of Worcester, Robertson and Swellendam.

The great chain of the Hex River mountains, continued under other names from west to east, divides the country into two different spheres of character, temperature, and productions. On the coast side are extensive divisions, containing groups of productive, well-watered valleys, raising a prolific yield of grain, wine, brandy, dried fruits and tobacco. Away above, on the plateau of the Karoo, there is the great silence of immense plains, bounded by low hills, on which, at far intervals, farmhouses are found. As in India, so in South Africa, the mountains dominate the land, and there are immense subterranean treasures of water. The rivers which occasionally pass through these plains are merely drains, but their waters can be retained by irrigation works. The soil is most fertile, and could be made to produce grain for all South Africa. The fruits, where there is water, are of the best quality, and it is not too much to say that the Karoo will yet become one of the greatest treasures of the Cape Colony. Many persons are singularly attracted by the dry, pure, health-giving air of this plateau, which, indeed, may be called great, as it extends west to east from Calvinia to Middelburg, and south to north from the Zwartbergen to the Orange River, thus embracing an area which considerably exceeds 100,000 square miles. The best sheep walks in South Africa are here, and it is probable that the finest agricultural farms may yet exist, when the science of irrigation is practically applied to elicit the generosity of Nature.

There are great rivers in South Africa, but none of them are navigable. The Orange carries at times a volume of water estimated at 50,000 tons a minute, but frequently dwindles into a fordable stream, although it rises in the Drakensbergen, drains, with its tributaries, more than 300,000 square miles, and flows for 1000 miles from east to west, until it falls into the Atlantic Ocean. A glance at a map will show that the southern portion of the continent is too poor to do without railways. They are an absolute necessity because of the want of means of water transit, and the mining centres have enabled lines to extend from the ports to Johannesburg in the Transvaal. In the west, we find a well-pastured country in the greater part of Damaraland, where there are vast herds of native cattle, but Namaqualand is a land of desolation, relieved by the richest copper mines in the world. 'The Kalihari Desert' is somewhat of a misnomer, as in it are found many farmers who find both water and good pasturage for their flocks, but portions of it are desert seas, with waves and billows of sand.

The eastern portion of South Africa far surpasses the western, as the highest mountains, the most fertile valleys, the greatest forests, and the best sheep country are here. Forest, mountain and lake scenery combine to make George and Knysna districts most picturesque and beautiful. The great primeval forests extend thence in an easterly direction to Humansdorp, and in them herds of elephants are still found. An immense extent of bush country is to be found still further east, and in the Addo Jungle, near Port Elizabeth, which extends inland for a distance of sixty miles, with an average breadth of twelve miles, not only elephants, but buffaloes and countless herds of wild deer (bucks) make this one of the best hunting areas in South Africa. There are two great features in the eastern province of the Cape Colony, or rather two sections of its territory, styled Karoo and 'Bush' country. One is specially suited for sheep, the other for cattle. Through great parts of those districts, this splendid banquet, spread by the hand of Nature, gives, not only to wild animals but to oxen and goats, both abundant supplies and adequate shelter. While, in the deep kloofs, carnivora still lurk, eager for their prey. Great chains of mountains stretch across, and to go up from any of the ports, is to ascend by gradations to levels varying from 3000 to nearly 6000 feet above the sea. After the bushy belt is passed, the Karoo is reached, or in the extreme eastern districts, rolling uplands and grassy basins and hills.

Going eastward, we find in the Transkeian territories, vast masses of an uncivilised, almost savage people. Polygamy prevails, and witchcraft has not yet been stamped out. This country and Pondoland are filled up with natives, many of whom periodically pour forth to take service at public works or with farmers. The great Drakensberg range of mountains form a north-western wall or boundary both to these countries and to Natal. The territories between them and the coast comprise good agricultural lands and excellent pastoral districts, while the charming scenery and genial climate secure comfort and health to the inhabitants. The coast lands of Natal present beautiful scenes, where undulating country with sugar cane and forest are bounded by the sapphire blue of the Indian Ocean. In this lovely semi-tropical country there are abundant supplies of delicious fruit; sugar is a well-established article of export, and now the tea industry is becoming very successful. In the higher country, sheep and cattle farming are carried on advantageously.

The crown of South Africa is Basutoland, which contains the highest mountains in this portion of the continent, and therefore is the cradle of great rivers which flow into the Indian and Atlantic Oceans. The country is now densely populated by an industrious agricultural people, whose superabundant grain crops can scarcely obtain adequate markets.

To the northward there are the plains of the Orange Free State, where the little Republic, with its Volksraad in Bloemfontein, wisely administers the government of a country comprising an area of 70,000 square miles, with a population of 77,000 whites and 130,000 blacks, and an income of £200,000 per annum. The railway from the Cape Colony to Johannesburg passes over its vast plains, and considerably adds to its revenue. The prairies formerly covered with coarse grasses, over which herds of wild game formerly wandered, are now so altered, that sweeter varieties of pasture provide food for the sheep and oxen of the farmer, while, in the 'conquered territory,' acquired from the Basutos, immense crops of cereals reward the agriculturist.

Crossing the Vaal, we are in the country of the South African Republic, which Mr Gladstone declared should not be retained, 'even were it as rich as it was poor.' It has turned out that it contains treasures beyond the dreams of avarice, in the shape of the Johannesburg gold mines, from which more than 170,000 ounces of the precious metal are now produced each month. The yield of gold from the Transvaal alone now exceeds £5,000,000 per annum in value, while the great auriferous regions of Mashonaland and Matabeleland are beginning to rise above the horizon. It is through veritable golden gates that civilisation is entering Southern Africa.

The Transvaal Republic comprises an area of 114,000 square miles, at an elevation varying from 4000 to 7000 feet above the sea level, and the greater part of its surface consists of well-watered, fertile soils and rich grassy pasturage, while its mineral treasures comprise gold, silver, galena, copper, lead, tin, and excellent mines of coal. It is, indeed, a country worth fighting for. The white population is only about 80,000, and the coloured people number nearly three-quarters of a million. The government in Pretoria is really more an oligarchy than a republic, as a clique of prejudiced men, while grasping all the pecuniary advantages they can, at the same time refuse the franchise to the taxpayer and freedom to the people. No Catholic nor Jew can hold office in a state which vainly boasts of being free. Transitions must take place, and at last the real independence and liberty of the Orange Free State may be attained; but, if hope be too long deferred, a revolution is possible, and if this take place, the British flag may again wave over the public offices in Pretoria. Johannesburg is a great centre of 50,000 people, to which all railroads from all ports now converge. It is the centre of attraction, of wealth, and of speculation. The old Kaap fields at Barberton, with their normal quartz reefs, are again, however, being worked, and the railway to Delagoa Bay, which will connect them with the sea, is in course of completion. Swaziland adjoins, and is a mountainous, pastoral mining country, under the sway of ill-conditioned savages, who protest very loudly against being handed over to the tender mercies of the Transvaal Boer.

British Bechuanaland is a very sparsely-peopled Crown colony, chiefly consisting of undulating prairies generally devoid of bush, but in exceptional cases dotted over with trees and patches of forest. A magnificent country for cattle ranches. Land varies in price from 1s. to 4s. 1d. per acre. The area of this territory comprises 60,000 square miles, and the population amounts to 6000 whites and 55,000 coloured people. The Bechuana Protectorate is an enormous extension. There we behold 386,000 square miles, covering country between the Shashi and Macloutsie, and the important Tati gold fields, where are the excellent Blue Jacket and Monarch reefs. Well-watered and fertile regions, fine pastoral country, and also tracts which embrace the Kalahari Desert, and other regions where it seldom rains. Khama's territory is within it, where Christianity has had the effect of putting an end to polygamy, and to the sale of intoxicants to natives. Already the great trunk line from the Cape Colony has reached Mafeking in British Bechuanaland, and this railway should be extended over 400 miles of easy country to Tati, and thence across an intervening distance of 120 miles to Buluwayo.

It is impossible to describe the various climates, soils, temperatures and productions of the vast country, comprising nearly a million square miles, ruled over by the British Africa Company. The area of France, Germany, Austria and Italy all combined is far surpassed in size by this new and gigantic empire recently placed under the British flag. There are low districts, in which fever prevails; there are great high plateaux, such as Gazaland, which are magnficent countries for the agriculturist and stock farmer, where both men and the lower animals enjoy a salubrious and delightful climate. Vast tracts can be covered with the best rice in the world, and coffee can be grown to an unexampled extent with every prospect of success. There is no product of nature almost which cannot be raised; and the mineral treasures of Rhodesia—the real foundation of all material prosperity for the Company—are such, that in a short time the last El Dorado will be proved to be one of the richest. The evidence on this point is very conclusive, although it is not desirable to refer to it more fully here. Certainly there is no instance since the discovery of America in which greater opportunities have been offered than those now given to the civilised world through the efforts of men who, while attending to their own interest, throw open vast fields for energy, capital and labour. Mineral centres have revolutionised South Africa. They created railways, markets for farmers, and general prosperity, when the diamond mines of Kimberley were found. The discovery of the Johannesburg 'Banket' reefs opened up a new era, not only for the Transvaal, but for the Orange Free State and the Cape Colony: while now the gold of Rhodesia is stimulating railway extension from every port, and will form a very powerful factor in the work of consolidating various and varied interests. A consummation devoutly wished for is the assimilation of customs duties, railway tariffs, postal and telegraph regulations, with free trade between all sections, so that it may be practically, if not in name, 'the United States of South Africa.'

The expansion of the congerie of countries south of the Zambesi has really only commenced. The Cape of Good Hope has been the Rip Van Winkle of colonies, which went to sleep in the seventeenth century, and only awakened to real life and action when diamonds were discovered at Kimberley in 1870. All the other states are of yesterday, and can be looked upon as children with a great career before them. A few statistics will make this clear. Here are one and a quarter millions of square miles, comprising a larger territory than British India, with a population of five millions, including only six hundred and seventy thousand people of European extraction. Imports of the annual value of £14,000,000; exports, £15,000,000; and in the latter case we must calculate that gold amounts to more than £6,000,000, and diamonds to nearly £4,000,000. Here is indeed room for the overflowing populations and energies of the old world. Every natural advantage of climate, soil, pastures and mineral wealth! The story of the expansion of the past can be written in a small volume, but history now is made in the southern hemisphere so rapidly, that the time is not far distant when our chronicles, like our prosperity, will expand. In the meantime, this contribution to the history of the beginnings of an empire is respectfully laid before the public.

# The Story of the Expansion of South Africa

―o―

## CHAPTER I

*Early History—The Hottentots, Bushmen and Kafirs —Customs, Manners and Characteristics*

FOUR hundred years ago Southern Africa was unknown to the civilised world, except in mystic fable or obscure conjecture, to-day it is one of the most flourishing and prosperous regions in the southern hemisphere. The adage that 'there is nothing new under the sun' finds exemplification in the fact that the most ancient gold mines in the world have become its most modern 'diggings'—the 'Ophir' of King Solomon reappearing in the rich auriferous fields of the Transvaal and of the Chartered British South Africa Company.

Diamond mines of unexampled wealth yield gems to the value of about four million pounds sterling per annum, the copper mines of Numequeland are in richness second to none in the world. But when we consider the vast extent of these territories, and the fact that they have only been very partially explored, it is not too much to say that the immense mineral treasures of the South African Republic, Swazieland and Matabeleland are, as it were, merely rising on the horizon. We are only beginning mineral discovery in South Africa, and, day after day, hear of new mines of gold, iron, silver, coal, tin and quicksilver. Our sheep walks and cattle runs are not surpassed in excellence anywhere, enormous tracts of irrigable land await cultivation, the wheat of the Cape Colony is of first-class merit, and Southern Africa can be made one of the granaries of the world. In this vast section of a vast continent, extending for thousands of miles in length and in breadth, comprising all the country from the River Zambesi to Cape Agulhas, there are, of course, a variety of climatic conditions, but, speaking generally, Nature has crowned all its benefits by a delightful, exhilarating and healthful climate. The existence of the coloured races is an immense benefit, as, by means of them, cheap labour is obtainable, and large agricultural supplies can be constantly procured; but Southern Africa, although its population chiefly comprises the descendants of stalwart nomadic races who have migrated from a northern portion of the continent, is eminently a white man's country, where homes can be found for millions of the overflowing populations of Europe.

Four hundred years ago a few Hottentots and Bushmen dwelt in the country between the Great Fish River and Table Mountain, and the fierce Kafir nations were in course of migrating in a southerly direction, but had scarcely reached the present confines of the Cape Colony.

The history of South Africa, preceding the arrival of the first European navigators, is shrouded in mystery. We are told by Strabo that the Phœnicians sailed down the Red Sea, doubled the Cape of Good Hope, and then sailed up the African coast, so as to reach their own country by the Straits of Gibraltar. There is better evidence that in the ninth century the Arabs were acquainted with the coast as far south as Delagoa Bay; and now we find by discoveries at the ruins of Zimbabye and other forts in Matabeleland, that a people of Asiatic extraction[1] worked for gold in mines at a period so remote, that native tradition even can give us no information respecting them. In the south of the continent there were Hottentots and Bushmen. The language of these people was essentially the same, and was a pure form of the ancient Coptic tongue of Egypt. At least, this is the confident opinion of Dr Bleek,[2] who devoted his life to the study of the subject. According to his theory, the Bosjesmans of South Africa are identical with the pigmies of Herodotus, and these people, together with the Hottentots, to whom they were allied, have by degrees, through many centuries, been driven southward by more powerful tribes, until at last Table Mountain and the ocean became barriers to a further migration. If this be so, we have no trace whatever of any aboriginal races of Southern Africa.

The Dutch Settlers necessarily came in con-

[1] See Bent's explorations, likewise Works of Selous. The latter by no means agrees with Mr Bent, and advances good arguments in favour of the opinion that the ancient gold workers from Asia took wives in the country, and eventually became a portion of the native tribes of the continent.

[2] Librarian of the Grey Collection South African Library. His work on the native languages of South Africa is very valuable. His conclusions are not admitted by Dr Hahn and other writers.

tact with Hottentots, and the latter were, so far as we know, the earliest inhabitants of Southern Africa. They styled themselves Khoi-Khoi—'men of men,' and were originally a powerful nation divided into tribes, each of which was presided over by a chief. Their riches consisted in flocks and herds, with which they roved about seeking pasture, and carrying with them in their migrations moveable villages, each hut of which was composed of poles or boughs covered with rush mats. Their clothes consisted of sheepskins, and their weapons of bows and poisoned arrows. Bold and active in the chase, they were courageous in danger, although naturally of a mild and gentle disposition. Intellectual gifts, as well as the qualities of humanity and good nature, were possessed by them. Kolben, who lived among them at the beginning of the seventeenth century, when they were uncontaminated with the vices of civilisation,[1] declares that 'they are perhaps the most faithful servants in the world.'

They were, however, 'dirty in their habits, slothful and indolent; and, although capable of thinking to the purpose, hating the trouble of thought.' The Hottentots, like most savages,

[1] The present State of the Cape of Good Hope, by Pieter Kolben. See also *Le Vaillant* and *Thunberg*.

were spiritualists, as they paid special reverence and attention to the departed spirits of their ancestors. The dread of the influence of spirits was so great that on the death of anyone, the kraal in which he or she expired was immediately removed to another position. They are said to have believed in a Supreme Power, termed 'Gounza Tekquvä,' or 'God of all Gods,' as well as an evil Deity, represented as an ugly, ill-natured being, styled Toutouka. The most singular religious custom of these savages was their veneration for a particular kind of insect (Mantis), whose help they implored when in peril or suffering from hunger. The Bushmen were of small stature, and dirty yellow colour, with repulsive countenances, in which there was a prominent forehead, small, deeply-seated and roguish eyes, with a much depressed nose, and thick projecting lips.[1] Dissolute in habits, clothed in sheepskins, dwelling in low huts, or circular cavities dug in the ground, which scarcely defended them from the weather, they seemed to form the lowest grade of the human race. Nevertheless they have left drawings and paintings in their caverns

[1] An excellent description of the Hottentot Race is given by Adolph Bonatz, quoted in the *Cape Monthly Magazine*, Vol. III. p. 35.

which indicate intelligence of a superior description, while their Coptic language and apparent knowledge of hieroglyphics[1] lends countenance to the idea that they were original inhabitants of Egypt, and have degenerated through ages of persecution. Certain it is that they were the most deadly and hated enemies of the Dutch settlers. Quarter was never given, and so far from any attempt being made to bring them under the influence of the Christian religion a war of extermination was always waged against them. True, they were clever, irritating, and continual thieves. As far as they possibly could they persistently lived on the flocks and herds of the farmers, and these men at last were rendered so desperate that towards the close of the eighteenth century a

[1] Barrow thus describes some of these drawings (*Travels in Africa*, Vol. I. p. 193) :—'The different antelopes that were there delineated had each their character so well delineated, that the originals from which the representations had been taken could without any difficulty be ascertained. Among the numerous animals that were drawn the figure of a Zebra was remarkably well executed; all the marks and character of this animal were accurately represented, and the proportions seemingly correct. *Several crosses, circles, points, and lines were placed in a long row as if extended to express some meaning.*' See on the disputed question of the Coptic origin of the Hottentot-Bushman languages Dr Bleek's *Comparative Grammar of South African Languages* (1869), and Hahn's *Grundzuge Einer Grammatik des Hereros*, Berlin.

war of extermination was successfully waged against the Bushmen. The Hottentots did not disappear in the Cape Colony until a late period of the nineteenth century, and brandy was the chief agent in removing them.

The Kafirs of South Africa, in contrast to the Hottentots, have increased and multiplied, and at the close of the nineteenth century are more numerous than at any previous period. While there are forty thousand people of European extraction in Natal, the Zulus of that colony exceed four hundred thousand in number. In the Cape Colony, according to the last census (1891), there were Europeans or Whites, 376,812; other than European and White (coloured races), 1,148,927—the latter bearing a proportion of 75 per cent. to the entire population. In Bechuanaland, Basutoland, Zululand, the South African Republic, the Chartered Company's territory and the Protectorate, there must be more than two millions of coloured people, so that it will be readily seen that at the present moment Europeans form only a fraction of the population of Southern Africa. The recent discovery of great mining centres is increasing the number of Europeans, but the native question commands attention as one of the problems whose solution not only affects the well-being, but even the very existence of white domination. At the outset, therefore, it is very desirable to ascertain the nature and characteristics of those great races, generally termed 'Kafirs,' which must continue to comprise an overwhelmingly large proportion of the population of Southern Africa.

Ethnically the Kafir races form a well-marked variety of the negro type, and unquestionably a distinct branch of the Bantu family. They comprise a fine tall race of men, some of whom are jet black and others a dark copper colour. Their features are often fine, with the forehead well developed, and, both physically and mentally, they are greatly superior to the negroes of the west coast. It is erroneous to class them as of the same race with Hottentots and Bushmen.[1] One of the great authorities on the Kafir tongues divides them into two great classes—the 'Click,' and the 'Alliteral.'[2] He tells us

[1] Such a good authority as Dr Keith Johnson does this. It is noticeable that Dr Livingstone never attempts to place the Kafir and Hottentot in the same category.

[2] *Introductory Notes to a Kafir Grammar*, by the Rev. J. W. Appleyard. Warren's epitome of the Kafir manners and customs published under the authority of the British Kaffrarian Government, is the most valuable and reliable work on manners and customs of the Kafirs in the Cape Colony; it is entitled, *A Compendium of Kafir Laws and Customs*. The Reports of

that the particular origin of these languages has yet to be discovered, and thinks that it may probably be found among the tribes which occupy the interior regions to the south or south-west of Abyssinia. 'On many accounts there are good grounds for supposing that they are of Ishmaelitish descent, and consequently that they are of the same origin as many tribes of Arabia.'

Their government is an admixture of feudalism with Patriarchic customs. The Amapakate (middle ones), or council, is a powerful check upon arbitrary power. Its members give military service whenever called upon, and in return receive a share of spoils, and are invested with civil jurisdiction in their respective neighbourhoods. Each of them has his own followers and partisans. Every crime is punishable by a fine; and as *persons* are the property of the chief, penalties for acts of personal violence

---

Commissions and Blue Books of the Cape Colony and Natal comprise voluminous details. *Kafir Folk Lore* has been written by G. M'Call Theal, and in that writer's *History of the Boers* there is a great mass of information respecting native tribes. Information can be obtained from the innumerable books of South African travel. The most interesting and valuable of the old works are Sir John Barrow and Burchell's *Travels*, written at the beginning of this century. Kolben is unreliable, and so is Le Vaillant, although written at a comparatively early period they are worthy of special attention.

and murder are received by him. As the legislative, judicial and executive departments are confounded, justice cannot be efficiently administered. There is neither a fixed code of laws nor any constitution or system of legislation. Lawless and predatory habits are considered praiseworthy, while the prospect of gain and the desire of revenge are ruling passions and motives of conduct. There is no definite fixed idea of God. Some of the more thoughtful among them have some vague idea of a Supreme Being, but the national belief extends no farther than the ghosts or spirits of their departed chiefs or warriors, and, in some instances, those of their ancestors in general. To the ghosts of the departed they attribute all the powers ordinarily ascribed to the Deity.[1] Witchcraft is directly connected with this belief, and its practice is the chief—indeed the almost—exercise of belief among these people. It has had the most powerful effect on the history of South Africa, and as an illustration of this fact, it is only necessary to refer to the extraordinary disaster caused by it in 1857, when the incantations of the Witch Doctor Umhlakaza induced the Kafirs to destroy their cattle, in order that,

[1] See *The Past and Future of the Kafir Races*, by the Rev. W. Holden, p. 283.

having, as it were, burned their boats, a desperate war of extermination could be waged by them against the hated European intruders. A girl was used as a medium, and she professed to hear strange and superhuman sounds in the earth under her feet, which eventuated in solemn and peremptory instructions from the spirits that the people should destroy their cattle and their corn so that they might rise again with vast increase, and that their enemies might be defeated and flee before them. Sir George Grey, the Governor of the Cape Colony, knew all this, and took the necessary precautions, so that the only result was that 70,000 Kafirs died of starvation, and the British authority became more firmly established. Nothing more devilishly cruel than witchcraft exists in the world. A rapacious chief, with equally rapacious counsellors, covets the herds and wives of a wealthy man. As a means to obtain possession of them, ' smelling out' by a witch doctor is resorted to. The victim is charged with having caused some illness or disaster by means of incantations. In vain the unfortunate man begs for death. This is never granted until, for many hours, generally for days,[1] he has been subjected to the most

---

[1] Godlonton, in his *Narrative of Kafir Wars*, graphically describes current instances of witchcraft torture. In one in-

inhuman and revolting tortures. From this Europeans have saved the natives, and civilisation can plead that if this alone were the result of its progress, it would be more than sufficient for its justification.[1]

Among the Kafir races land is the property of the entire tribes, and individual titles cannot exist. Women are degraded to the lowest level, and by their social system classed among beasts of burden and the goods and chattels of

stance, a man, innocent of everything but having numerous cattle, is stretched bound on the ground, while large red-hot stones are kept upon his stomach so as to burn into his intestines. In other cases victims were burnt very slowly to death by being stretched above slow fires. Another torture, by which an English artilleryman, who was taken prisoner, suffered death, was smearing the body of the victim, tying him to a post beside a nest of ants, and leaving him to be slowly devoured by these insects.

[1] As illustrative of the superstitions of the native tribes of South Africa, handed down from father to son, we subjoin an extract from the work of a very recent reliable writer personally known to the author of this work :—' We were favoured with a visit from a wise man, who bore four peculiar-looking tablets in his belt, which he used for purposes of divination. He threw them and told the fortune by the way they fell, what side was uppermost, etc. This superstition extends among all the native races. In the colony there are people who pretend to be able to give information about lost or stolen cattle, as well as cure diseases, tell what is going on in distant places, etc. One Commandant of Police had so much faith in one of these wise men that he made him always accompany him in his inspections and patrols. A brother and a nephew of the writer were once on the way to the Diamond Fields when they lost their oxen, and when all hope of recovering them had been given up, one of

her master. Polygamy, of course, is universally allowed, and under a system of purchase the number of wives bears proportion to the wealth of the husband. Concubinage is permitted, while the vilest and most degrading immorality prevails.[1] One of the most com-

these wise men informed them where to look for them, and they were recovered in the place indicated. An ex-member of the Legislative Council of Natal once informed me that he was greatly struck with a narrative told him by a person in whom he could believe. This man was a complete disbeliever in native conjuring, and happened, when travelling, to be at a place where a wise woman, by certain charms and incantations, gave him minute information about where his waggons were and what had happened on the journey. When they arrived he found that she had been perfectly accurate. He still went on, however, in a very rude manner declaring that she was a humbug, until the woman became enraged and said,—"White man, you asked me for certain information. I gave it. What I told you was correct, and you abuse me. For this I curse you!" She then foretold that his oxen would die on the journey, some of the people would lose their lives, and others would desert him. All happened as she predicted, and the man was ruined.'
—*Through Matabeleland*, by Joseph Garbett Wood, M.L.A., London, 1893.

[1] Gross immoralities are legal at certain times. Warren's *Manners and Customs*: Holden (*The Past and Future of the Kafir Races*, p. 288) thus refers to witch doctors' operations which came under his own observation, and with which he was familiar,—'Before the approach of the suspected person, the witch doctor, without any apparent knowledge of the parties, from whence they come, or what is the nature of their mission, foretells their approach, and by means not of spirit-rapping or clairvoyance, but of spirit-speaking, professes to declare what is transpiring, and it usually happens as he has prognosticated. Those persons who seek to account for these mysterious revela-

petent and best-informed writers on the customs and manners of the Kafir races[1] tells us that marriage among the Kafirs has degenerated into slavery, and that among them not only is seduction not punishable, but no disgrace whatever attaches to it. It is noticeable that this

tions without assigning them to supernatural causes, intimate that this knowledge is acquired by various persons and agencies employed by him for the purpose. There is, however, much greater difficulty in explaining these phenomena by these ordinary means than by supernatural interposition. . . . In order that a spirit may reveal what is required, the witch doctor "takes bundles of sticks and assegais, the tails of beasts, and the skins of snakes and wild animals, and ties them about all the parts of his body; also the feathers of ravenous birds, which he fixes in his hair . . . performs the most frenzied gesticulations, utters the most unearthly sounds, until the scene becomes a very pandemonium, the council chamber of demon spirits, the hall and assemblage of infernals."[1] Among the Zulus the victim is not only killed, but his wife and children also, while all his property is seized. Warren, in his Kafir *Manners and Customs*, pp. 89 and 90, tells us that 'In the Bush country, where the tree ants are plentiful, their nests are sought for, the poor wretch is laid down, water thrown over his body, and the nests beaten to pieces on him. This irritates the ants, and causes them to bite furiously; they also creep into the nostrils, ears, eyes, mouth, etc., producing the most excruciating pain by their bites. Sometimes a large fire is made, and the poor wretch is tied up to a pole, so close to it as literally to roast him alive. Large flat stones are also heated red hot, and placed on the groins, and applied to the soles of the feet and other parts of the body.' As regards divination by means of throwing bones, and the extraordinary accuracy of predictions which came under his own observations, see Col. J. G. Wood's recent work, *Through Mashonaland*.

[1] Warren, *ut supra*.

is also the case both with respect to theft and drunkenness. The bold robber of cattle is second only in merit to the successful slayer of men. Truth is not known as a virtue, while lying and dissimulation are the weapons of diplomacy.

We have referred to the salient features of Hottentot and Kafir character, laws and customs. It is now necessary to trace the history of the gradual conquest of these savages by people of European extraction. The history commences as far back as an early period in the seventeenth century, and the warfare still goes on, although the position now gained is the mastery of that part of the continent which extends from Capetown to the Zambesi. A wonderful expansion of the realm of civilisation has taken place, and it is our object to chronicle the slow and gradual steps of the first Dutch commanders, the more assured progress under British rule, and last, but principally, the wonderful march of events since the discovery of diamonds in the year 1870 to the defeat in 1894 of the greatest native power hitherto unconquered in Southern Africa. The record is one of absorbing interest and importance. The foundations of a great nationality have been laid. The Afrikander race has arisen, and what must yet take rank as one of the principal empires of the southern hemisphere begins to demand the attention of the world.

# CHAPTER II

Early Portuguese Discovery—Diaz and Da Gama—Dutch and English visit the Cape—The Dutch East India Company forms a Settlement—Van Riebeek the first 'Commander.'

THE grand ambition of Prince Henry of Portugal[1] was the prosecution of maritime discovery, and to the furtherance of this object he devoted all the energies of his life. The progress of discovery was gradual. Madeira became known in 1418, an expedition sailed round Cape Nun in 1433, and at last, in 1440, Cape Blanco was reached. Nuno Tristan doubled Cape Verd in 1446, three of the Azores were seen by Gonsalez Vallo in 1448, and some years afterwards Portuguese vessels anchored off the shores of

[1] As to life of Prince Henry, see Barros, and *Vido do Infante Don Henrico*, by Candido Lusitano, translated into French by the Abbé Cournaud. An excellent *Life of Prince Henry*, by Major, published in London, can be easily consulted. In one of the treatises prefixed to Mickle's Translation of the *Luscad* (Vol. I. p. 47), it is stated that Prince Henry always professed that, 'to propagate the Gospel was the great purpose of his designs and enterprises. Certain it is, that the same principles inspired and were always professed by King Emmanuel, under whom the Eastern world was discovered by Gama.'

Sierre Leone. Diego Cam reached 22° south latitude in 1484, and a few years previously Pedrao de Caralhas had gone from Egypt to the Red Sea, and thence to the East Indies, and back to Sofala on the East African coast, so that there was every reason to believe, 'as well for the reason of the thing as from the concurring opinion of the seamen conversed with,' that a short and easy passage might be found round the continent of Africa to the Indies. The acquirement of riches, the extension of Christianity, and specially the destruction of the monopoly of Eastern commerce enjoyed by the Italian Republics, were the ruling incentives to Portuguese maritime discovery. So ardent was the desire to reach India by sea, that to effect this object no labours were considered too arduous and no dangers too great.

There is an analogy between the discovery of America and of the passage round the Cape to India. It was in the same city (Lisbon), and almost in the same year, that both schemes were concerted. Both projects had the East Indies in view as an ultimate object, Columbus merely finding the American continent in his endeavour by a western route to reach India. Columbus opened a new world to mercantile enterprise,

but Diaz and Da Gama unlocked the gates of a new highway to the regions of the old world. Columbus was supplanted by Amerigo Vespucci, and Bartholomew Diaz by Vasco Da Gama. Both were unfortunate, and treated with ingratitude while living, though commemorated and honoured after death, as if Honour's voice could

> 'Provoke the silent dust,
> Or flattery soothe the dull, cold ear of death.'

It was in the year 1486 that three small vessels under the command of Bartholomew Diaz doubled the Cape of Good Hope, and on the 14th of September of that year took shelter in Algoa Bay, after having previously anchored at Angra Pequina, and set up a cross there. So many gales were experienced, that the southern promontory, near which they had suffered, was styled by these mariners the 'Cape of Torments;' but subsequently the name of Cape of Good Hope was conferred on it by 'John, the second king of Portugal, for that hope which he conceived of a way to the Indies.' Diaz returned to Lisbon in 1487, sailed subsequently to Brazil, and at last, on the 29th of May 1500, found a mariner's grave off that Cape of Storms, of which he had been the first European discoverer. The glory of finding the new highway is his; the southern ocean into which he led the way is his grave, and the Cape which towers above it his monument.

Vasco Da Gama sailed out of the Tagus on the 8th of July 1497 in command of a little fleet of small vessels, manned by only 160 men. When we consider that they knew full well what storms and difficulties had been experienced in the previous voyage of Diaz, and that they had to penetrate further into unknown seas, we cannot but admire the heroism of these mariners, whose deeds are worthily commemorated by the greatest Portuguese poet, who sings of—

> 'Arms and the heroes, who from Lisbon's shore,
> Through seas where sail was never set before,
> Beyond where Ceylon lifts her spicy breast
> And waves her woods above the watery waste.'[1]

---

[1] *The Lusiad of Camoens*, translated by Mickle. The voyage must have seemed strange and adventurous, as even the sky above changed during their progress so as to present to them new stars and constellations.

> 'While nightly thus the lonely seas we brave
> Another pole star rises o'er the wave;
> Full to the south a shining cross appears,
> Our heaving breasts the blissful omen cheers—
> Seven radiant stars compose the hallowed sign
> That rose still higher o'er the wavy brine.'

St Helena Bay, on the west coast of the Cape Colony, was reached on the 7th of November 1497. We are told that the natives appeared to be small, black and ugly; their voices were disagreeable, and the weapons they used were made of 'wood hardened in the fire, pointed by the horns of animals.' On even the first occasion of meeting, Europeans endeavoured to overawe the natives. Two pieces of ordnance were fired off in order to strike terror, and we cannot, therefore, be surprised to read that a fight shortly afterwards took place in which Da Gama was wounded. It is added that this commander afterwards 'made himself dreaded whenever the treachery of the natives provoked his resentment.' Mossel Bay was afterwards visited by the expedition, and on Christmas Day more easterly shores were sighted, and named Tierra de Natal, in honour of the Nativity.

The storms are specially referred to—

'To tell the terrors of the deep untried,
What toils we suffered and what storms defied;
What mountain surges, mountain surges lashed,
What sudden hurricanes the canvas dashed.'
*Lusiad*, Book IX.

'With such mad seas the daring Gama fought
For many a day and many a dreary night;
Incessant labouring round the stormy Cape,
By bold ambition led.'—THOMSON.

The Portuguese did not think it worth while to establish any settlement on the shores of the stormy Cape, and England followed this example. The half-way house to India became only a primitive post office, where letters were frequently left for the commanders of ships.[1] Various visits were made by the ships of several nations. M. De Gonneville and the French ships under his command experienced a fierce storm off the Cape of Good Hope, while Francisco D'Almeida, Count of Abrantes, first Viceroy and General of Portuguese India, was killed by Hottentots on the Grand Parade, Capetown, where the General Post Office now stands.[2] The English ships under Captain James Lancaster anchored in Table Bay (then called Saldanha Bay) in 1591, and for upwards of ninety years Portuguese ships almost monopolised the carriage of spices, silks and other

---

[1] Pedro de Nueva, for instance, is recorded to have found, in an old shoe on the Mossel Bay shore, a written description of the state of affairs in Portuguese India, addressed to him by P. de Alayde.

[2] *Camoens* makes the 'Spirit of the Cape' say—

> 'With trophies plumed behold a hero come,
> Ye dreary wilds prepare his yawning tomb.
> . . . . .
> Quiloa's sons and thine Mombaze shall see
> Their conqueror bend his laurelled head to me.'

The wizards of Cochin had predicted that he would never pass the Cape.

Eastern produce from India to Europe round the Cape of Good Hope. The Dutch had been unsuccessful in discovering a north-eastern passage from the European seas to China, and looked with extreme jealousy upon the success which had attended Portuguese enterprise. A Dutch merchant, who happened to be imprisoned in Lisbon, inquired diligently into the mysteries of Eastern commerce, and offered to some traders of Amsterdam, if his release were purchased, to communicate the precious information which curiosity and observation had enabled him to gain.[1] His proposals were accepted, and when set at liberty his revelations excited the men of Holland to an enthusiastic resolve. They were determined to have a share in the treasures of India. As a means to that end, a squadron of four ships was despatched under the auspices of 'The Association of Distant Lands.' These were the first Dutch ships which anchored in Table Bay. Numerous squadrons followed, and the Cape soon became a place of call for the vessels of

[1] See *Lectures on the Cape of Good Hope*, by Judge Watermeyer, p. 3. This is a very valuable and scarce work, embodying in an able and enlightened manner the philosophy of the history of the Cape Colony under Dutch rule. As authorities on early Cape history should also be quoted, *Verhaal der O. I. Compagnie*, Du Bois's *Vie des Gouverneurs General* and the *Cape Historical Annals*, translated by Moodie.

all nations. Davis, the Arctic voyager, was a visitor in 1607, and the Dutch Admiral Maaklof left a number of rams and ewes on Robben Island in the following year; Henry Middleton called in 1607, and Captain Sharpey in 1608. An abortive attempt was made by the English East India Company to establish a penal settlement at Robben Island in 1614, and in 1620 two English captains, named Shillinge and Fitz-Herbert, after a consultation, on the 3d of July 1620, erected the British flag on the shores of Table Bay, and declared that they took possession of the country in the name of King James. Their principal arguments in favour of taking and keeping the Cape were, ' That this great country, if it were well discovered, would be kept in subjection with a few men and little charge, considering how the inhabitants are but naked men, and without a leader or policy'; that the Dutch, who evidently intended to form a settlement, would be shut out ; and that the British fleets on the Indian route 'might be refreshed.' No attention was paid to these mariners, and it was not until the beginning of the nineteenth century that the supreme importance of the Cape as a strategic position was recognised. Indeed, South Africa up to a very recent period has been a Nazareth, from which it was presumed no good could come; but numerous recognitions have been forced upon the world. About the beginning of this century, Lord Malmesbury was compelled to declare that, 'If the French are masters of the Cape and Trincomalee we shall hold all our settlements in India and the Isles of France and Bourbon entirely at the tenure of your will and pleasure; they will be ours only as long as you choose we shall retain them; you will be sole masters in India, and we shall be entirely dependent on you.'[1] No part of the southern hemisphere has been so slow in having its merits recognised as the Cape Colony and adjacent territories. It was comparatively *terra incognito* until diamonds were discovered in 1870. A wild country, troubled with ferocious savages and constantly recurring wars, offered few inducements to emigrants, but the discovery of immense mineral treasures, like a magician's wand, has entirely changed this position, and regions which export gold and diamonds annually to the amount of more than ten millions pounds sterling are now regarded with respectful attention by the world. Nor is this all, or nearly all, for this is specially a land

---

[1] Quoted by Barrow (Sir John) in the first edition of his *Travels in South Africa*.

of good hope, and we shall see that only the
beginning of still greater epochs, marked by
even greater successes, is probably before us.

A book by Sir Thomas Herbert[1] introduces
us to the Cape in 1626, and we notice it because of the decisive manner in which he sums
up the characteristics of the Hottentot race.
According to him, they were inveterate thieves.
'The cattle they sold us, had they not been
secured by tying their heads to some stakes,
would break after the savages upon one man's
whistle.' They were thoroughly deceitful, untrustworthy and perfidious.[2] In fact, if his
opinions be accurate—and there is little doubt
of it—we are furnished an explanation of a
great portion of subsequent history. As in the
case of the Hottentots, so in that of the Kafirs,
people in Europe, who possess no real practical

[1] *Travels by Sir Thomas Herbert.* There is a copy in the South African Library, in which among the plates is a representation of Table Bay where the mountains are named Herbert's Mount, The Table, Sugar Loaf and King James's Mount.

[2] Sir Thomas Herbert says, 'To sum up their character with that which Salvian *libro de vero judicio* gives of other Africans when he says they are "inhumani, impuri, ebriosi, falsissimi, fraudulentissimi, cupidessimi, perfidissimi, et obscœnis, libidinum omnium, impuritati et blasphemiis addictissime," etc.; and for a farewell take that which Leo gives the Libyans, "They have no letters, faith nor law, living (if it be a life) like wild beasts for ignorance, like devils for mischief, and like dogs for poverty." This scarcely accords with the nonsense written by Voltaire about the "noble savage."'

acquaintance with their character and conduct, have blamed colonists frequently in a most sweeping and unjust manner for acts in which, had they themselves been in their place, they would undoubtedly have participated. We will see in due course how much evil this description of injustice has done, both to natives and Europeans. A due knowledge of savage character and conduct is absolutely necessary for the student of colonial history who desires to judge impartially.

In the year 1648 the ship *Haarlem* was wrecked in Table Bay. Two of the seamen on their return to Holland addressed a memorial to the directors of the Dutch East India Company, strongly urging the establishment of 'a fort and garden' at the Cape of Good Hope. As the Chamber of Seventeen had in 1619 adopted a resolution in favour of this proposal, very little was now needed in the way of information and advice to induce them to carry it into execution. Accordingly, three ships, named the *Dromedary*, *Heron* and *Good Hope* were fitted out, and on the 5th of April 1652 Surgeon Van Riebeck, who commanded the expedition, 'got sight, God be praised, of the land of the Cabo de Boa Esperanza.' On the 7th of April they anchored beside 'the Fresh River,' and when a boat's crew went ashore, a box of letters was found, left by Jan Van Teylingen, the commander of the homeward-bound fleet.

On the 9th of April 1652 Von Riebeck assumed the government of the embryo colony. Exactly one hundred and sixty-eight years after, on the 9th of April 1820, the first ships bringing British settlers to the Eastern districts anchored in Algoa Bay. Seventy years subsequently diamonds were found at Kimberley. During the twenty-four years which have since elapsed, the auriferous treasures of the Transvaal have been thrown open to the world, and to-day we chronicle the overthrow of the last and greatest savage power of South Africa by the British Chartered Company. The importance of the history of this portion of the continent is in converse ratio to the lengths of the periods into which it can be naturally divided. There was comparatively little progress or prosperity in the first long period just alluded to. An improved but not much accelerated ratio is traceable in the second; but in the third the rate of progress was entirely changed, and more was done in twenty years than had been effected in the previous century. Now we have entered upon a time when the expansion of Southern Africa is taking place so rapidly that books can be written upon the exciting events of even one year.  Such being the facts, it is evident that, in spite of the comparative length of the first two periods of our history, it is out of the question to treat them in detail.  Indeed, the chronicles of the Cape commanders concerning the trifling events of an infant settlement need only be briefly alluded to.  The stream of Cape history is not only very tiny at its commencement, but it remains exceedingly diminutive for very many years.  The settlement was a petty one even when conquered by the English in 1806, and under such circumstances, it is neither desirable nor necessary to do more than refer to interesting events illustrative and indicative of the character of the people, the policy of the Government, and the beginning of that expansion so heroically carried on subsequently by the Voortrekkers.

The sole aim of the Dutch Company in forming a settlement at the Cape was to establish a place of refreshment for their ships, both outward and homeward bound.  The cultivation of vegetables, and acquiring cattle from the natives were, therefore, among the principal duties of the new Government.  A little fort was built, barter with the natives commenced, and everything possible was done to keep the Hottentots in good humour. The instructions from the Company very sensibly enjoined that any quarrel with them should be avoided. This was merely, however, the result of expediency, as we find Commander Van Riebeck lamenting that he was prohibited from seizing ten or twelve thousand head of cattle, and sending their owners to India to be sold as slaves. In the early records there is a good deal about the observation of religion, but in reality it is difficult to find much to admire in the opinions and conduct of the Governors. When a French ship anchored in Saldanha Bay, efforts were made to get the seamen to desert, and, with the utmost duplicity, an attempt was made to lure the captain to Table Bay in order that his ship might be destroyed.[1] On the 19th of October,

---

[1] In a despatch from Van Riebeck he excuses himself for liberality to foreign ships on the ground that much of the beef he sent on board was unsound. To give an idea of the number of vessels that visited Table Bay at this time, it may be mentioned that in 1656 forty-four called, thirty-five of which were Dutch, five English, and four French. One of the principal Dutch explorers was Jan Huyghen Van Linschoten, whose first book, published in 1595, gave us an account of Portuguese maritime discovery near the Cape of Good Hope. His description of India was published in 1596. Linschoten's

when long religious services were being held, the first cattle raid took place, when a large number of cattle were carried off by the Hottentots. This robbery was perfectly unprovoked, and is only an illustration of the fact that savages are perpetually thieves. The cause of countless subsequent native wars was the cause of the first one—the theft of cattle. As this forced the labourers to eat unpalatable penguins instead of good beef it made them extremely exasperated—but they had to bide their time. They were not yet strong enough to attack the Hottentots. These children of nature were soon shrewd enough to notice that brick had replaced wood in the European building, and that extensive gardens were in course of being cultivated. They objected to any permanent occupation of any portion of their pastures, and as a protest against it built their huts as close as possible to the fort. Soon there was not sufficient ground at Table Bay for the stock of the Company and of the

map of South Africa is one of the curiosities of cartography, the true source of the Nile in great lakes in the centre of the continent is accurately shown. On the east coast of South Africa there is one magnificent river, and east of that, all is 'Monomotapa' thickly dotted with towns. Hakluyt's *Principal Voyages, etc.*, London, 1599, and Purchas, *His Pilgrimage*, London, 1625, give narratives of the first English voyages to the East.

Hottentots. The latter, therefore, were ordered to move. Their reply was that the ground belonged to them. The Commander answered that the Company had taken possession of it. Later on the unfortunate natives suffered heavily from not being able to graze their cattle on the rich herbage at the foot of the mountains, but knowing the superior weapon of the white men they feared to attack them. They adopted instead a system of guerilla warfare, carried on by means of systematic and continuous theft. At last the Burghers could tolerate this state of matters no longer, and called upon the Government to protect them. The usual fighting by proclamation and religious utterances followed.

'The true object of attacking their enemies was not booty in cattle, nor revenge—for that belonged to God alone,' etc., etc. A few savages were killed on this occasion, and a treaty of peace was soon afterwards entered into. By degrees, as the settlement increased in strength, a firmer attitude could be taken and was assumed. In 1671, natives who were caught in the act of sheep stealing were brought to the fort, soundly flogged, branded, and sent to Robben Island. The astute Commissioner, Overbeck, who visited the Cape about this time, thought it would be expedient to make a formal purchase of the country. The Hottentot chief applied to consented very readily, for the excellent reason that by this bargain nothing was taken from him which was not already lost. By this pompous and utterly absurd agreement, still preserved in the Registry of Deeds Office, Capetown, the whole district of the Cape, including Table, Hout and Saldanha Bays, is sold in perpetuity to the East India Company of Holland. Goods to the nominal value of four thousand reals of eight (£80) is given in exchange. In a despatch to the Directors the value of the goods actually transferred to the natives is put down at £2, 16s. 5d. Of course, this was a dishonest bargain, dishonestly carried out. The land already was in possession of the Company, the seller had no choice whatever, and even the value in goods stipulated was not paid.

During Van Riebeck's time expeditions were sent into the interior. The Paarl Mountain was named and the little Berg River discovered. The Namaques even were found out, and an expedition under Jan Danckert set out for 'Monomotapa.' Imported slaves were sold on credit at prices varying from £4, 3s. 4d.

to £8, 6s. 8d., and when, at the end of ten years, Commander Van Riebeck was ordered to Batavia he left a little vegetable and cattle-raising settlement firmly established for the refreshment of the fleets of the Dutch East India Company. He was very anxious to be removed, and was treated unjustly by his strict taskmasters in Holland, who grumbled about the settlement having to import rice. They declared that they saw no advantage in a country which could not produce its own food, and were of opinion that farmers were badly wanted at the Cape. In 1661 his term of office expired, and he went off gladly to the Dutch El Dorado of the East, Batavia, and Mr Zacharias Wagenaar ruled in his stead.

# CHAPTER III

Events under Dutch East India Company Rule—The History of a Narrow Monopoly—Arrival of Huguenot Emigrants—The Rule of the Van der Stells—Shipwrecks—Capture of French Ships in Table Bay—War with the Hottentots and Bushmen.

An expedition was sent by the Dutch against Mozambique, intercourse with Madagascar took place, and the island of Mauritius became a dependency of the Cape. Van Quaelberg and Borghorst succeeded Wagenaar, and harsh regulations were considered necessary for the Hottentots. It is noticeable that about this time, 1671, the country about Mossel Bay was surveyed and a little liberty to trade was accorded to the Company's servants. Amid the dreary, tiresome and most diffuse *Annals of Dutch rule*,[1] which have been carefully preserved and virtually republished at full length, we find occasionally something that is

[1] *Annals of Cape of Good Hope*, by Moodie, *History of the Cape Colony* (Wilmot and Chase), *History of South Africa*, and *Chronicles of Cape Commanders*, by Theal, go into the minutest details, and are all monuments of patient labour.

dramatic, which can be read with interest. On the 9th of May 1660 the French ship *Marechal* put into Table Bay, and on the 19th of the same month was wrecked in a heavy northwesterly gale. The Governor of one of the French Factories at Madagascar, together with a Catholic bishop and three priests, were among the passengers saved. A proclamation was issued, without loss of time, prohibiting all religious services in the settlement except those of the 'Dutch Reformed Church,' so that these poor shipwrecked strangers were not allowed to worship God in their own manner. The bishop, it is said, was a man of great wealth and good family, who had exchanged a career of dissipation for a life of sincere piety. He had devoted himself to Madagascar missions, and, although this was the third time in which he had in vain sought that island, he nevertheless determined to charter a ship on his return to Europe, and again tempt the perils of the sea.

Pieter Hacknes succeeded Borghorst, and he in his turn gave way to Van Brengel, Isbrand Goske, Johan Bax, Van Herentals and Hendrik Crudop. 'The Wee Wee German Lairdie' is a type of these insignificant commanders of an insignificant settlement. A stone fortress was built on the shores of Table Bay which, strange to say, was considered impregnable, although in an absurd position commanded by the neighbouring heights. The census of 1679 showed that the inhabitants of the settlement comprised 142 free men and women, 117 children, 30 European men-servants, and 191 slaves. It was in this year that Mr Simon Van der Stell, a clerk in the office of the Chamber of Seventeen, was appointed commander. His wife declined to go to such a savage region as South Africa. On his arrival he found the little colony comprised only a few settlements round the foot of Table Mountain as well as a cattle station at Tygerberg, and outposts at both Hottentots Holland and Saldanha Bay; but in his time, during twelve years, it spread over the lovely and fruitful country, bounded by the mountains of Drakenstein and Hottentots Holland. It must be admitted, however, that the Dutch had already begun to show their trekking propensities, and that the interior had been explored as far eastward as George, and as far northward as forty or fifty miles beyond the Oliphants River. Stellenbosch, named after the Commander, was established, and tree planting on a comparatively large scale was commenced. In August 1683 an expedition was sent into Namaqualand, and the fame of its copper mountains were the chief attraction, but so barren and desert was the country, that the explorers were forced to return without penetrating into these rich mineral regions. The Commander himself subsequently visited Namaqualand, but although he ascertained its great wealth, these treasures of copper were never mined until after a lapse of nearly two hundred years. The Cape Copper Mining Company during the latter part of the nineteenth century has been reaping a harvest which was ready for the sickle under the rule of the Netherlands Company.

The rule of the Dutch Company at the Cape was that of a narrow monopoly. There was neither freedom nor pretence of freedom. Trade belonged to the Government, and was its perquisite, and any permission to traffic given to the burghers was an exceptive indulgence. The mere desire of a place of refreshment for ships only required a very small garrison, whose principal duty was to cultivate gardens and obtain oxen for the outward and homeward bound fleets. There was no desire at first to obtain a large accession of territory; but, nevertheless, certain tracts of ground near Table Bay were required for pasture, and in a cunning manner, as has been described, nominal purchases of land were made from the native tribes. But after the first quarter of a century of possession there was no affectation on the part of the Dutch authorities that native claims to land should be respected. Thus the land of Waveren, subsequently called Tulbagh, was soon added, and—the authorities sometimes preceding the inhabitants, more frequently the colonists preceding the authorities—possession was taken from time to time of the lands to the north and the east, until the arid wilderness northwards and Kafir defiance eastward formed the boundaries of European encroachment.[1]

Nothing can be plainer than the course followed. The native tribes were, in the first instance, so powerful that conciliatory measures, and the ostensibly fair means of obtaining land by purchase had to be adopted. The Dutch soon gained strength in proportion as the Hottentots, enervated by European vices and frequently defeated, became weaker and less able to resist. What at first was advisable soon became unnecessary, and land was

[1] So says Mr Justice Watermeyer, whose eloquent lectures on the early history of the Cape of Good Hope form one of the most important contributions to the study of the subject. The lectures of Mr Justice Cloete on early history specially bearing reference to Natal are valuable.

annexed without form or pretext, as convenience dictated. The early colonists and the Government were strongly opposed to shedding blood, except in defence ; and at first prudential reasons contributed to this feeling. Indeed, ' for the greater part of the first century of the Dutch occupation the life of the black man was as sacred as that of the white, and the atrocities at which we shudder, of the men who hunted down Bushmen like wild beasts, were reserved for the end of the last and the commencement of the present century.' [1]

It is remarkable that no effort worthy of the name was ever made to civilise the natives. Christianity does not seem to have been considered fit for Hottentots, while the Bushmen thieves, whose slaughter we shall have to chronicle, were regarded as mere outcasts and pariahs, to be shot down like wild beasts.

In the little settlement the term ' Cape Freeman' was a misnomer. The Commander and the Grand Council of Polity exercised the inconsistent functions of the Executive, the Legislature, and the Supreme Court of Justice, so that they could constitute any act a crime, and then punish it. There was, it is true, a right of appeal to the Indian authorities at Batavia,

[1] Mr Justice Watermeyer.

but woe betide the man who dared to exercise it. The current ran smoothly until the Huguenot emigrants were introduced, and then rather dramatic proceedings command our attention.

The revocation of the Edict of Nantes caused an exodus of Protestants from France, and they became so numerous in the Netherlands, that in the year 1687 the Dutch East India Company saw the possibility of sending detachments of them to the Cape. They knew that in their settlement the vine grew luxuriantly, and they were desirous of sending men out whose knowledge of vine culture and wine making would enrich the settlement. One hundred and seventy-six Huguenots were sent out.[1] Although treated with kindness, they commenced to grumble shortly after their arrival, and continuously disturbed the Government with their grievances. Their manner of location and being forced to form a portion of a Dutch congregation, became subjects of complaint. When a deputation waited upon the Commander at the castle, and on behalf of their

[1] Within the following twenty years various families followed, but never more than two or three at a time. The total number of Huguenots who came to the Cape could not have exceeded 300. They had to give up their language. Numbers of Boer families now bear French names. Theal, in his *History of South Africa*, publishes elaborate lists, and furnishes the most minute details.

countrymen requested permission to establish a separate church, the Governor flew into a rage, and declared that the French were the most impertinent and ungrateful people in the world. They were, in reply, reminded of their oath of allegiance, and commanded to return to their homes. The Dutch colonists evidently took the part of the Government, as many among them refused to hold intercourse with the new-comers, and said that they would rather give bread to a Hottentot or to a dog than to a Frenchman. Some years afterwards, in the time of the younger (Willem Adriaan) Van der Stell, the sparks of discontent to which we have just referred were fanned into a dangerous fire. Petitions were sent to Holland complaining of the unrighteous and haughty tyranny of the Governor, that he avariciously had seized upon the best lands, filched cattle from burghers, excited the Hottentots to commit injuries, and numerous other offences. The clergyman also is attacked, and charged, amongst other things, with being from home when children were brought to be baptised. The brother of Van der Stell is referred to as being 'as full of mischief as an egg is full of meat.' This 'younker' is charged with having, at the Governor's desire, bribed several men ' to assault and cudgel two ancient burgher councillors, so that they should feel it.' Two petitions, couched in the strongest language of invective, were sent—one to Batavia, and the other to the Chamber of Seventeen. An opportunity of forwarding the latter to Holland was being sought when Van der Stell received intelligence from Java that the petition had reached the Governor-General of India. An investigation took place, which in a small community could scarcely fail of being successful. Adam Tas was found to be the ringleader, and he was immediately arrested, while his papers and books were seized. Vigorous measures were taken to secure the traitors, but those that avowed they were misled were offered pardon, if they would come before the authorities and declare their repentance. Those who chose discretion as the better part of valour were treated to tobacco and copious draughts of beer, while the wicked and malicious inhabitants, who had issued libellous documents and seduced others from their virtuous courses, were told that, in default of speedy repentance, they were to be treated as seditious mutineers. The French refugees, and the later Dutch colonists were the malcontents. Nine recusants fled into the interior, and were pursued by mounted soldiers, but in vain.¹ The Governor certainly did not consider himself guilty, as he banished several of the mutineers to Holland, and these men lost no time in obtaining powerful friends and securing an order for the recall of Van der Stell. The home Government did not evidently believe that Van der Stell had been guilty of the atrocities laid to his charge, as he was expressly allowed to retain his rank and pay. It was evidently recognised that very ample authority had been placed in his hands, in the exercise of which errors of judgment were committed when dealing with men of turbulent and discontented character, who did not scruple to exaggerate greatly, and bring charges, many of which could not be proved.²

[1] One of the refugees is referred to in a book published in Holland in 1713 as having escaped from the French King's Dragoons, and arriving at the Cape as to a safe retreat, to find that the Governor as well had Dragoons at his command, and through whom he could make the place intolerable.

[2] Numerous pamphlets, teeming with abuse, refer to Van der Stell's administration. Of course he had his friends, who published replies. He does not seem to have been quite the monster he is made out to be by his enemies, as Van der Marre the poet sings his praises, and abuses the discontented burghers in *Eer Kroon Van de Kaap de Good Hoop*. Van der Stell became celebrated in Holland for his devotion to literature and science. He is referred to by Burmann as the *Praestantissimus*

The history of the Cape Colony is interspersed with narratives of shipwreck. At one time a Portuguese, at another time a French ship are lost on the coast, and in many cases the survivors suffer much from exposure and long marches. Few of the Dutch East India Company's vessels left their bones on the rocky shores of South Africa. The *Stavanesse*, however, was an exception. On the night of the 16th of February 1686, in calm weather, the look-out reported that he saw land, but the officer of the watch knew better, and declared that it was mist. Presently the roar of the surf was heard, and the vessel went to pieces on the coast, seventy miles south of Natal. Eleven of those on board were drowned, and sixty souls reached the shore alive. Three officers, who, unable to travel, were left behind in a tent, and fifty-seven men determined to reach Table Bay by a march overland. Ten of these soon became fatigued and abandoned their companions, but the remaining forty-seven went boldly

*Botanophilus*, as a Governor who did much for natural science when at the Cape. It is very significant in favour of Van der Stell, that long afterwards, when the writing-desk of Adam Tas was opened, under Governor Van Assenburgh, the Council of State appointed a committee to examine the documents in it, and it was reported that some of them were seditious. These were destroyed, and the others returned to Tas, who called his estate 'Libertas,' as a punning way of declaring that Tas was now free.

along. The men left behind were, after all, better off than the others, as two Englishmen came to visit them, who had lost their vessel in the preceding year within the Bay of Natal. They had been living for nine months with the natives, and knew their language so well as to induce them to conduct the party from the wreck to Natal. Other Englishmen were there encountered, and, by united effort, a very seaworthy little vessel, which they named the *Centaurus*, was built. In this they successfully sailed to Table Bay. The authorities there were naturally very anxious about the fate of the forty-seven men, and sent out the staunch little ship to search for them. Off the Cove Rock, near the mouth of the Buffalo, a small raft was seen with three naked men upon it, paddling towards the vessel. These were part of the unfortunate crew of the *Stavanesse*, who stated that there were on shore eighteen others. Out of this number fourteen were rescued. Subsequently, two or three of the remainder were found by the *Noord* when she touched in at Natal during an exploration of the east coast. We are told that among the first party rescued was a French boy, who was the only survivor of a boat's crew which had attempted to land on the coast.

The Portuguese ship, *Nostra Senhora de los Milagros*, struck on the rocks between Agulhas and False Bay on the 16th of April 1686. The night was beautiful and perfectly clear, but the master of the ship, being confident that he had rounded the Cape, set no watch, and steered directly on shore. Three ambassadors from Siam to Portugal were on board, besides a good many other passengers, and a crew of more than 200 men. So contracted were the real limits of the settlement at this time, that those who succeeded in reaching the beach could obtain no food, and were in despair. The eldest of the Siamese ambassadors died of grief and distress shortly after reaching land, and such sufferings were endured by the survivors in the short march to Capetown that many of them died in consequence.

As the Siamese did not appear, a sergeant and six soldiers were sent to look for them, and found them wandering about among the mountains—still alive, although a month had elapsed since the shipwreck.

Diamonds to the amount of £100,000 was the only treasure saved out of this unfortunate ship.

Among the few events of interest which grace the early Cape annals, the capture in

Table Bay of the French ships, *Normande* and *Coche*, stands prominently forward. War had been declared by the King of France against the United Netherlands, and it was known at the Cape in March 1689 that all Dutch ships in French harbours had been seized. All this was, however, unknown to the captain of the French ship *Normande*, homeward bound from Pondicherry with a valuable cargo, which put into Table Bay on the 6th of April 1689. According to custom, he sent a boat with a complimentary message, but the crew were made prisoners when they got ashore, and Dutch sailors dressed like the Frenchmen whom they had replaced, and still keeping the French flag flying, pretended to put off as if on the return journey. The deceived *Normande*, when adding to her former politeness by firing a salute, was boarded by the crews of Dutch ships in port, and after a short scuffle, in which no one was killed, the ship was surrendered. The captured ship was used as a bait, and her national flag kept flying, so as to delude her consort, *La Coche*, to follow her course and share her fate. The latter, in due course, entered the Table Bay trap on the evening of the 5th of May, and lost no time in saluting the Dutch flag with nine guns. She then sent off a boat to the *Normande*, but as this did not return, and a large Dutch ship was observed to be coming up, the captain (D'Armagnan) called to quarters. The *Nederland* then poured in a destructive broadside at close quarters, which killed the brave French commander and three of his crew, besides wounding eight others. Five hostile ships were now around their victim, and therefore surrender was compulsory. Fifty thousand pounds was the value of the cargoes of the two prizes, which were renamed the *Goede Hoop* and *Afrika*. They were sent to Europe with the Company's homeward-bound fleet, while the prisoners, 140 in number, were forwarded to Batavia.[1]

The Chamber of Seventeen considered that the Cape had become more important, and, consequently, the officer administering the government ceased to be a commander, and

---

[1] In time of peace the French had been courteously treated by Simon Van der Stell—so much so, that he had received a present of a gold chain and medal, as well as a portrait of Louis XIV., in return for civilities. In June 1685, an embassy to Siam put into Table Bay in a French ship. Six Jesuits were on board, including in their number two of the best astronomers of the time, to whom the pleasure house at the Company's garden was granted as an observatory.

became a governor. Nevertheless, the advance of the country was very slow, and thoroughly unsatisfactory. A state of torpor, broken by frequent discontent, had now become its normal condition. The state of the country was due to the false principles on which the colony had been founded. The attempted union of a mercantile factory of a monopolist nature, with a mongrel free colonisation system was a signal failure. A mere place of refreshment might have answered the wants of the Dutch traders; and if this plan had been rigidly adhered to, there would then be neither any colony nor any hope of prosperity in South Africa; but possibly the native owner of the soil would not have been despoiled. On the other hand, had the European colonists not been fettered, but allowed the free development of their energies —free commerce and free cultivation—it is lamentable that the process of the extermination of the black man might have been more rapid. The theory, which has been carried into practice in South Africa, as in America, that while the coloured races are supposed incapable of prosperity in close contact with the white, the white shall be deemed entitled to seize on all the land of the coloured races, would perhaps have received even yet more terrible and universal application, but the country would not have lost a century and a half of progress.[1]

After the Van der Stells[2] passed away, Van Assenburgh and William Helot followed. Then came Mauritz Pasques, Marquis de Chavonnes, a French Huguenot nobleman, who ordered that the statutes of India should form a code of laws for the colony. About Pieter Gysbert Noodt, who began to hold the reins of government in 1727, there is quite a halo of romance. A German tutor, who lived in the colony

[1] These are the sentiments of Mr Justice Watermayer upon the history of the early history of his own country, expressed in his Lectures.

[2] Simon Van der Stell, after whom Stellenbosch and Simon's Bay were named, resigned his appointment, and retired to his farm 'Constantia,' where he had built a handsome residence. He died in June 1712, and his remains were buried in the church of Table Valley. His son, who succeeded him in 1699, had been for ten years an official in Amsterdam. A very interesting narrative is given of the wreck of the *Bennebrock* on the coast of Natal in 1713. The survivors remained for several months on the coast, and when they tried to go westward, were stopped by great rivers. They went inland afterwards, and eventually only seven survived, who found refuge with a tribe of natives, who were constantly at war with Bushmen. Here they found a Frenchman, who had been wrecked thirty years before. Eventually one sole survivor of the *Bennebrock*—a Malabar slave—reached the Breede River, and was brought to Capetown.

One of the most dreadful gales on record was that which visited Table Bay on 17th June 1722, when every ship in the bay—ten in number—was wrecked, and 660 men perished.

towards the middle of the century, weaved a story about this unpopular Governor which is also to be found in several other narratives. It is stated that, having condemned some men unjustly to death, one of their number, on the scaffold, called upon Van Noodt to appear before the judgment-seat of God, and that, when the execution was over, the obnoxious Governor was found dead in his arm-chair. It seems that the facts are that the Commander was ill-tempered and disliked; moreover, he was found dead in his chair, and he had previously, with the council, condemned to death—justly, according to the laws of these days—several men who had deserted with their arms and robbed the guardhouse. Everything else is untrue, which shows what calumny can do, and how careful we must be in believing many statements which are handed down as historical facts.

A little expansion had taken place, although, up to the year 1743, there was only one seat of magistracy outside of Capetown, and that was at Stellenbosch. Lower Breede River, soon styled the division of Swellendam (in honour of Governor Swellengrebel), followed, but even then it was declared that a greater number of people than the existing small population could not obtain a living in the country, unless free exportation of produce was permitted. The rule of Ryk Van Tulbagh for twenty years—from 1751 to 1771—was, however, favourable to progress; at least it was long considered the golden age of Cape administration, and this Governor has been constantly praised for his wisdom and benevolence. One of the most enterprising parties which had ever proceeded inland was despatched, under Ensign Bentler, which penetrated to the eastern districts, and through them to Kafirland. The Keiskamma River was then justly considered to be the boundary between the Hottentots and Kafirs. The former then occupied a vast, fruitful, and beautiful country. One hunded and forty years have passed away, and where are they? Gone like the autumn leaves of past years, with the exception of comparatively few at the Kat River settlement. The expedition from the Cape claimed all the country for the Company, and at various places raised up beacons as tokens of sovereignty. A special one was built at the mouth of the Zwartkops River, in Algoa Bay, and attention was paid to the principal bays on the east coast. In 1755[1] there were 5510

[1] The shipwreck of the English ship *Doddington* took place in this year on a rock now called after her, close to the Bird Islands, off the eastern shores of Algoa Bay. On this occasion,

colonists and 6279 slaves in the settlement. A
quaint and peculiar state of society then prevailed, in which extreme conservatism prevailed. The sumptuary laws of Dutch India
were put in force, and regulations which now
seem to us absurd existed, such as those providing that every person, without exception,
should stop his carriage and get out of it when
he saw the Governor approaching; that only
persons of certain rank should use large um-
brellas; and that silk dresses were not to be
worn, nor embroidery used, by any ladies except
those of the upper class. Even the number of
servants and horses that every individual might
have was regulated, and the Placaat followed
burghers even to the grave, and prescribed
rules about strewing dust before the house
door as a sign of bereavement.

The Bushmen, the Hottentots, and the
Kafirs were the natural enemies of Europeans

247 persons perished, and the survivors—twenty-three in number—eventually built themselves a sloop, which they called
*The Happy Deliverance*, and escaped in it to Delagoa Bay,
where they found ships, which carried some of them to India
and others to England. There is a romance connected with a
treasure in a cave at Woody Cape, the promontory near the
Doddington rock, which has been made the subject of a drama.
The legend is that a Dutchman, when in this cave, saw a large
number of men, dressed as sailors, issuing from the back of the
cavern, diverting the channel of a small stream, digging in its
bed, and bringing up a dozen iron chests of treasure.

in South Africa. The first-named, inhabiting mountains and deserts, carried on war with the others, and, like the wolf on the fold, came down whenever possible on the flocks and herds of the settlers. The Kafirs were invaders of the Hottentot country, and, if tradition be accurate, defeated their enemies early last century in a great battle on the Kei River, and drove them westwards. So far as the Dutch colonists were concerned, their great plagues were the little crafty Bushmen, who drove the cattle of Pieter Laubser from his farm in the Bokkeveld in 1763, and killed numbers with poisoned arrows, visited a cattle station on the Zak River in 1764, and there murdered the European servant and stole 300 sheep. On this last occasion their retreat was discovered, and twenty-three of their number killed. In May 1770, they drove a herd of cattle from a farm in the Karoo, and later in the same year many farms were plundered. These are specimen occurrences merely. Raiding, pursuing and killing went on steadily. A commando under Van der Merwe killed 142 Bushmen, but this officer afterwards made peace, for which he was severely censured by the Government. The war of extermination was vigorously continued, and we find that Commandant Van

Jarsveld in 1775 killed no fewer than 122 Bushmen. The manner in which he carried on operations is so significant as to command our special attention. He tells us that they proceeded to the upper end of the Seacow River, when they met unawares one of those cattle plunderers, and also saw a great many of these thieves at a distance. 'In order to create no suspicion in the mind of the thief that we had caught, we behaved peaceably to him in order to get the other thieves in our power.' He was told that they came as friends, was regaled with tobacco, and told to go to his friends and offer them peace. Seacows were killed to further entice the Bushmen. The bait attracted the victims, upon whom the Dutch fell suddenly at daybreak, and slaughtered every savage who was there with the exception of five, who managed to escape. All this is set forth in Van Jarsveld's *Journal*,[1] and is evidently looked upon as highly creditable and praiseworthy work. In spite of many commandos, the Bushmen were so numerous in the neighbourhood of the Sneeuwbergen (Snowy Mountains Graaffreinet) that many farmers were forced to leave that neighbour-

[1] *Van Jarsveld's Journal* (he was Landrost of Stellenbosch), August 4th to August 10th.

hood. Petitions for assistance resulted in orders for the destruction of this hated race. Continual patrolling and offers of land as reward for killing Bushmen were of little avail. At last, in 1787, a very strong commando, divided into five parties, was sent out by the Landrost and military court of Graaffreinet, with orders 'to destroy that pernicious nation,' and the Landrost of Stellenbosch was ordered to co-operate. Again, in 1792, an expedition under Van der Walt scoured the country between Tulbagh and Zak River, with the result that 158 Bushmen were killed and 51 taken prisoners. It is recorded that between the years 1786 and 1795 no fewer than 2480 of these people were killed, but in that very period they had stolen from the farmers 617 horses, 17,633 cattle, and 77,176 sheep. The Landrost of Graaffreinet (Maynier) tells us in 1792 that every year large commandos of 200 or 300 Boers 'had been sent out against the Bushmen, and learned by their reports that generally many hundreds were killed by them, the greatest part helpless women and innocent children.' He goes on to say that, to prevent such atrocities, he stopped the commandos and substituted other measures, the result of which was that the depredations of the Bushmen nearly ceased. They were certainly crushed in such a manner as to give comparatively little trouble in the future. At the close of the eighteenth century the Hottentot and Bushman enemy was fairly well disposed of, but the Kafir had risen on the horizon, and had to be dealt with.

# CHAPTER IV

*The Baron Von Plettenberg—Local Discontent—Naval Engagement between English and French Fleets—The Heroism of Waltemade—The Loss of the Grosvenor—Expansion of the Colony — Establishment of New Divisions—State of the Colony—Arrival of Commissioners of Inquiry—War between the French Republic and the Netherlands—The Prince of Orange requests the Colony to submit to Great Britain—Arrival of the British Fleet—Miserable and Discontented State of the People—Surrender of the Colony to the British Crown.*

THE Prince of Orange appointed Van Plettenberg Governor of the Colony, and he assumed office in May 1774. Extension of territory becomes discernible in the naming of a bay on the east coast after this functionary, while almost at the same time the eventual northern boundary of the colony was styled the 'Orange River' by Captain Gordon. The Great Fish River was now declared the eastern limit of the settlement, on the same principle that the painting of the African map with the colours of various European nationalities goes on at the present day. No better men than the

Dutch could have come to the Cape of Good Hope, so far as a restless spirit of 'trekking' is concerned. There seemed an innate desire for the patriarchal life, where, undisturbed by taxes and restrictive laws, they might live in calm peacefulness and comfort. Isolated farms soon sprung up in very distant places, and we will soon see what very remarkable effects are traceable to this movement. The petty discontents and troubles of a petty settlement do not require much attention. The Government was styled tyrannical by the burghers, and the people were stigmatised as seditious by their rulers. As a specimen of grievances, the case of a man named Carel Hendrik Buitendag can be referred to. He was a drunkard, who behaved so brutally to his wife that she prayed for a separation, and so shamefully to his family, that the Landrost of Stellenbosch, with his Heemraden, petitioned for his forcible removal. The Government acceded to the request, but twenty days after the application had been made, and when the man was behaving himself, the domestic quarrel being forgotten, he was seized by black scavengers, dragged through the town, placed on board ship, and taken to Batavia. His wife and children had now changed their minds, and followed to the beach lamenting. The unfortunate man, when he reached India, obtained leave to return to the Cape, but died on the homeward voyage. The deportation of Buitendag became a magnificent pretext for indignation, and 400 burghers applied through three delegates to the Council of Polity for leave to elect persons to be sent to Holland to lay their grievances before the Company. This was refused, but the Council expressed its willingness to hear complaints and redress grievances. Nevertheless, the malcontents subsequently sent delegates to Europe, and their complaints were very carefully heard and thoroughly investigated. Of course they were sent for report to the Governor, and it must be admitted that the explanation of Van Plettenberg and the high officials at the Cape show that the grievances were not nearly so great as they had been represented. The Governor was disgusted with the people, and requested his recall. The only result of all the complaints was the eventual displacement of the Fiscal or Public Prosecutor, who was evidently too conservative for even the Chamber of Seventeen, and an alteration in some details of administration.

Local discontents had now to be put on one

side, as on the 30th of March 1871, the French frigate *Silphide* arrived in Table Bay, bringing the news that on the 20th of December 1780 war had been declared by Great Britain against France and the United Provinces. Ships were ordered to Saldanha Bay, the burghers declared that they would fight to defend the colony, and great excitement prevailed. On the 20th of May 1781, the French frigate *Serapis* brought the news that a French fleet with a large number of soldiers might soon be expected. On the 13th of March 1781, an English fleet of forty-six sail, with 3000 troops, under Commodore Johnstone, had sailed from Spithead for the conquest of the Cape. A battle was fought with the French fleet under Admiral Suffren, off St Jago, when our fleet was taken at a disadvantage and suffered severely. Admiral Johnstone sailed to the Cape, but Suffren, with a strong fleet, was before him. The English Commodore had been hitherto rather unsuccessful, but now was more fortunate than he could almost have hoped. The *Active*, of 32 guns, which he sent in advance to reconnoitre, hoisted the French flag and spoke the Dutch East Indiaman *Held Woltemaade* in the French language. By this means full intelligence of the arrival and strength of Suffren's fleet was obtained. The tricolor was then hauled down and the old English Jack substituted, with a request for the surrender of the betrayed merchantman, which was at once acceded to; and thus not only a valuable cargo, but treasure to the amount of £40,000 was secured. When the *Active* returned and reported that the Cape was too strong to be attacked, Commodore Johnstone wisely turned his attention to five large Dutch East Indiamen at anchor in Saldanha Bay. The English fleet, flying French colours, sailed thither, but hauled up the British ensigns when they entered. The Dutch officers should then, in accordance with instructions, have immediately destroyed their ships, but in one instance only had the necessary preparations been made, and this vessel alone (*The Meddelburg*) was blown up. Four fine Dutch ships were captured, and the Commodore sailed back to England, taking them with him.

The people at the Cape were never done murmuring. In 1784, memorials were sent to Holland complaining of iniquitous government, and of the scanty attention paid by the home authorities to their frequent representations.

Some change was necessary, but evidently the Directors thought the alteration should be as much as possible in the direction of putting the Cape in a better state of defence. Lieutenant-Colonel de Graaf, an engineer officer, was therefore appointed Governor, and a large body of troops ordered from India. The complaints against Van Plettenberg had been as the idle wind blowing, as this official was never censured, and went to Holland in a triumphant manner as admiral of the homeward-bound fleet.

During the closing portion of the eighteenth century the trade of Holland seriously suffered during great naval wars, in which she no longer took a prominent and triumphant part as in the days of Van Tromp. The disasters to mercantile vessels on the South African coast were numerous, but there are only two noteworthy events of this period which must be specially referred to. These are the noble heroism of Woltemaade, and the loss of the ill-fated *Grosvenor*.[1] The great Indiaman *Jonge*

---

[1] The Cape was very well known and frequently visited. Captain Cook touched at Table Bay in 1772, and again in 1775. The French explorer, Kerguelen, visited Simons Bay, *en route* for the great Polar Sea, in 1773. The number of vessels which visited Table Bay in the years 1781-4 inclusive were, Dutch, 94; English, 38; French, 119; Danish, 62; Swedish, 22; Austrian, 48; Portuguese, 8; Italian, 2; Prussian, 13; Hamburg, 1; Russian, 3; Spanish, 1; and American, 1.

*Thomas* laboured terribly during a heavy nor'-westerly gale in Table Bay, and at dawn of day on the 1st June 1773, was driven ashore on the beach near the mouth of Salt River; the agonising sight of men calling in vain for help was heard by a poor dairyman, named Walraad Waltemaade, and full of pity for these unfortunates, he rode through the boiling surf and reached the ship's side. Two men held to the tail of his powerful steed and were safely borne to the shore. The experiment was repeated over and over again, until fourteen men had been delivered. But, unfortunately, the compassion and bravery of Waltemaade were greater than the strength of his horse. On the occasion of the eighth trial, the devoted man and his steed were conquered by the breakers and swept to destruction.[1]

The English East India Company's ship, *Grosvenor*, freighted with officers, civilians, tenderly-nurtured mothers and daughters, was approaching the dreaded African coast on a fine morning in August 1782. The shore was visible, but, as is so often the case, the officer

---

[1] The Dutch East India Company commemorated this act of heroism by calling one of their ships after the hero, and causing a picture of the scene of the rescue to be painted on the stern. On the occasion of the wreck of the *Jonge Thomas*, 138 men were drowned and 53 saved.

of the watch was careless, when suddenly the ship struck and the breakers came on board. So near were they to the beach that several men reached it on a hawser from the vessel. The wreck broke up, but a large portion on which many passengers had crowded drifted ashore, and 136 persons were saved and only fourteen drowned. Some provisions were washed ashore, and when these were collected the whole party set out for the Cape. From the first the natives proved unfriendly, the rivers were in some instances unpassable, the toils of the way and starvation were excessive, so we cannot be surprised to learn that only six sailors reached a farm close to Algoa Bay after having suffered the most acute hardships in a journey of 116 days. Who can estimate what the poor ladies and children endured?[1] No trace of any of the former has ever been found, and there is every reason to believe that they all died of fatigue and hunger. An expedition

[1] The great novelist, Charles Dickens, has, in a most affecting sketch published in *Household Words*, referred to the sufferings of the journey and to the tender kindness with which one poor boy was carried and watched over until he died. The names of the lady passengers were Mrs Hosea, Mrs James, Mrs Logie and Misses Dennis, Wilmot and Hosea. There was a rumour that some had been married to Kafir chiefs, but of this there is not the slightest evidence.

under Mr Jacob Van Reenen was sent to search for the survivors in 1790; but they could obtain no information, although the scene of the wreck and the country in the neighbourhood was visited, where they found three aged white women who were survivors of a wreck which took place not later than the year 1740.

Before the close of the century the great division of Graaffreinet was established, extending from Swellendam to the Fish River, and from the Snowy Mountains to the sea; and it was in 1785 that an old burgher resident in Stellenbosch was appointed to preside over it, while for the site of his public offices two farms were chosen almost girdled by the Sundays River near its source, where for generations the quiet inhabitants of one of the most important towns of the midland districts have been able to cultivate the finest grapes and fruits of the colony.[1] At a later period a por-

[1] Graaffreinet and Cradock are two leading towns of the Karoo districts, and their gardens prove that Karoo soil well watered is as productive as any in the world. The immense plains called Karoo, traversed by railways, are dominated by mountain ranges, and subterranean water abounds. There are many rivers which can be dammed. Undoubtedly, with irrigation, these extensive and barren-looking regions comprise great treasure grounds, on which enormous crops of the best cereals could be raised. In our expansion we have never yet had time to attend to this important subject, and consequently pay more than double the price that is paid for bread in Europe.

tion of this vast territory, which exceeded in size an average European kingdom, was cut off and named Uitenhage,[1] and this included the lower section on the shores of Algoa Bay. The Hottentots still held more real possession of the country than the distant Government, while very few farms occupied by the indomitable pioneer Dutch dotted an immense extent of country, which was chiefly used by innumerable head of game.[2] A patriarchal life was led by the few inhabitants, and cattle-breeding did not require much industry. Little was done to the land, and supplies were obtained by waggons which, laden with butter and soap, returned with the very few articles of food and of clothing which their simple life required. Self-reliance was inculcated by comparative isolation, broken by a fight for property, if not for life, with hated savages. To ride, to shoot, to endure privation, were all learnt in a school whose pupils developed into the brave voortrekkers of the nineteenth century, whose deeds we must yet chronicle. So far as Capetown and its neighbourhood are concerned, there was

[1] Named after a Barony of Commissary-General De Mist's in Holland.
[2] At least forty varieties of antelopes, as well as leopards, hyenas and other carnivora, quaggas, zebras, buffaloes, and hippopotami in some rivers then existed in the Cape Colony.

not merely comfort but luxury. The French troops which arrived in 1781 had introduced an expensive style of living, and now large, handsome houses, with costly furniture and many slave servants, superseded the plain dwellings of their fathers. So far did luxury go that the directors of the Company in Amsterdam complained about the Cape becoming a second Paris. Military expenditure caused money to be plentiful for a short time, but the prosperity was, of course, fictitious, and speedily came to an end. So far as the Government is concerned, it was far from successful in any point of view. The revenue was £28,000, and the expenditure £120,000 yearly. An incompetent Governor drew an immense salary in Capetown, and lived there in extravagance. A drunken deputy misruled Graaffreinet, and the inroads of the Kafir races were met by the very weak and foolish plan of buying-off and compromise. When these fierce hordes crossed the Fish River and claimed the country lying between that colonial boundary and the Kowie, a burgher commando soon collected and was prepared to drive them back; but the instructions to patch up a peace were imperative, and so, amid the indignation of the Boers, no attempt was made to retaliate, and not only were all the stolen cattle lost, but the prestige of the white man in the country was seriously injured.

Paper money not redeemable in specie proved necessarily a disastrous expedient, and became seriously depreciated. The Dutch East India Company itself was virtually in a state of insolvency, and, having to retrench everywhere, made no exception at its Cape settlement, where military outposts had to be abandoned, slaves reduced in number, certain mechanics and sailors sent to Batavia, and horses, vehicles, etc., sold. Governor Van de Graaff had displeased the Home Government, and was as unpopular with his employers as he was with the people over whom he ruled. He was recalled, and Commissioners General Cornelis Nederburgh and Simon Henry Frykenius appointed as Commissioners, under orders from the Stadholder of Holland and the directors, to investigate into the Company's affairs, and make all necessary reforms. These two officials only formed a portion of the Commission, which was appointed for all the eastern settlements of the Company as well as for the Cape of Good Hope.

The new Commissioners, who arrived in 1792, found included in their duties that of investigating into the continued dissatisfaction of the colonists, and it was not long before it became evident to their minds that no light task awaited them. The attitude of the burghers was revolutionary. At Simons Bay the local Council boldly withdrew a proclamation imposing a succession duty, which the directors had ordered to be levied. Public meetings were held, and the burgher councillors clamoured for leave to represent the people, which was at last ungraciously granted. The Commissioners were fond of fighting by proclamations, and publicly called on the people to retrench, and return to a simple style of living; and when they animadverted upon disloyalty, the people answered that they were faithful to the States-General, but opposed to the corrupt administration of the Company.

Certainly an example of saving was set by the Commissioners, as they came to the conclusion that the expenditure at the Cape should be reduced by the amount of £66,000 per annum. New taxes were levied, including a specially obnoxious auction duty. Properties were leased, salaries cut down, and eventually the yearly expenditure was reduced so as to only exceed the income by £27,000. Of course, the reduction of the garrison, and a general system of economy, caused considerable distress, and the prohibition of trade with foreigners was bitterly resented, and declared ruinous to the colonists. Then came the empirical remedy of a loan bank with a paper currency, whose results were, of course, disastrous. But the troubles of the Government were not merely those connected with finance and taxation; they had to deal with numerous tribes of thieving Hottentots and Bushmen, as well as with still more troublesome Kafirs. The last made bold inroads into the eastern country extending between the Fish and Sundays Rivers. Cattle were stolen, and in some instances farmers were murdered. 'Commandos,' both at Graaffreinet and Swellendam, advanced to the front, and Landrost Maynier, utterly detested by the Boers, was the representative of the Government, who made illusory treaties of peace with savages, and when called upon to report as to the causes of the war, blamed his co-patriots, and declared that the Kafirs were a peaceable, quiet people. The unfortunate Commissioners were beset on every side by trouble while endeavouring to secure peace at any price, with economy and retrenchment. To add to their sorrows, news arrived in 1793 that the French Republic had declared war with Great Britain and the United Netherlands. They enrolled all the clerks, Hottentots and half-breeds into military corps, and then were able to leave for Java, appointing (1793) Abraham Josias Sluysken to be Commissioner-General in their stead. The unfortunate Dutch East Indian Company, which had long been staggering under debt and difficulties, now fell so completely as to be forced to declare that its debt amounted to £10,000,000 sterling, that its credit was exhausted, and that the interest on loans could not be paid. A few feeble efforts were made in Capetown to increase the defences, but there was neither money to construct fortifications nor men to defend them. The people of the country districts, no doubt, felt the impotence of the Government, and revolutions occurred both at Graaffreinet and Swellendam. At the former place the inhabitants displayed the tricolor, and declared themselves 'Nationals,' showing that the contagion of the French Revolution had even spread into the South African Karoo.

In Swellendam, Paul Fouche, with nine armed burghers, interrupted the proceedings of the Session of Landrost with his Heemraden, and commanded the members not to leave the Drostdy. This South African Cromwell afterwards sent a message to the effect that his desires would be declared on the following day, and subsequently the officials were deposed, a new Landrost appointed, and a representative body, dignified with the title of a 'National Assembly,' established. The people of Stellenbosch sympathised with these fine doings; and as the entire military force in the colony only comprised 1200 men, whose chief duty was to defend Capetown, it was quite clear that nothing could be done against Republican patriots. It was just as evident that the Cape of Good Hope would easily and speedily fall a prey to a hostile power, and therefore the Prince of Orange, with whom Great Britain was in alliance, sent a letter, dated at Kew on 7th February 1795, ordering Commissioner Sluysken to admit the ships and troops of England as a friendly power into the colony. This missive was brought by a fleet under the command of Sir George Keith Elphinstone—the land forces on board under Major-General Sir James Craig. As the vessels of war comprised three ships of 74 guns, three of 64 guns, a frigate of 24 guns, and two sloops of war bearing a large military force, the request of the Prince of Orange became a demand that could scarcely be denied. There was a meeting of the Council of Polity, signals of alarm were made summoning the burghers to Capetown, and Lieutenant-Colonel De Lille was ordered to Simons Bay with 200 infantry and 100 gunners to strengthen a garrison of only 150 men. Of course, it was evident that no letter from an exiled prince in a foreign country could bind distant officials. Holland had, moreover, welcomed the French, remodelled the National Government, and abolished the office of Stadholder. The Council of Polity at the Cape could, however, only decline to submit. General Craig distinctly declared that his orders were to take the Cape, so that it could be retained until the restoration of legitimate authority in Holland. According to him, to decline British intervention was to declare in favour of the Cap of Liberty and of the guillotine.

Numbers of mounted burghers arrived from the interior. Even the disaffected 'National Assembly' at Swellendam sent a contingent. With such a force, however, there was little chance. There was none whatever, if the character of its commanders be taken into consideration. De Lille fled from the fort at Muizenberg immediately a shot was fired from the British fleet. The artillery camp was shortly afterwards abandoned, and the guns spiked. The land force of the invaders easily swept round the mountain, and, after a temporary check, met with a resistance from the burgher forces, which might have been serious if the regular troops had been well directed. So enraged were the Boers that they charged De Lille with high treason, and sent him under arrest to the castle. He was found not guilty, and possibly, as an Orange partisan, had determined not to fight against those forces which were acting in alliance with his prince. As reinforcements of about 4000 men arrived in the British camp early in August, there was really not the faintest chance of retaining the settlement. Nevertheless, the Burgher Council unanimously adopted a resolution that the colony should be defended to the last. The defending force of 1140 men melted away; a mutiny broke out in the Pandour corps, and a fleet of twelve Indiamen, with three British regiments on board, commanded by Sir Alured Clark, arrived in Simons Bay. An English force, about 5000 strong, marched from Menzenberg to Capetown; an absurd attempt at defence in the Wynberg camp was made, but, in order to save Capetown from being taken by storm, terms of capitulation were soon arranged, and on the 16th September 1795 the Dutch troops marched out of the castle and laid down their arms as prisoners of war. The terms of capitulation were fair and reasonable. No new taxes could be levied, old ones were to be reduced, private property was to be held sacred, and colonists were to retain all their privileges. The rule of the Dutch East India Company over the Cape now ended, after having lasted 143 years.

A narrow policy produced natural effects, and the infant settlement, constantly swathed in the tight swaddling bonds of monopoly and repression, did not expand as much in a century and a half of Company rule as it did in the following century during twenty-five years of liberty. True, in a geographical point of view, the colony had become greatly extended; but the Kafir was really master of the eastern districts, discontented and rebellious burghers held Graaffreinet and Swellendam, while so sparsely peopled were most parts, even of the western districts, that the country was

really only nominally occupied. Explorations
during the latter part of the century had been
chiefly directed to Namaqualand and Damaraland, but there nothing of a practical character
had been done. In fact, speaking generally,
the colony was in a miserable, discontented
and unfortunate position at the end of the rule
of a company, whose high aims and achieve-
ments were unfortunately ended in misfortune
and ruin.

# CHAPTER V

The New Government under Great Britain—Discontent and Rebellion—Missionary Enterprise—Kafir War—The Cape of Good Hope reverts to the Batavian Republic under the Treaty of Amiens—New Government incomparably better than that of the Dutch East India Company—Cape re-captured by Sir David Baird—The Battle of Blaauwberg—Rule of the British Government—The Earl of Caledon—Hottentot Missionary Difficulties—Another Kafir War—Murder of Landrost Stockenstroom.

ADMIRAL ELPHINSTONE with Generals Clarke and Craig carried on the Government in as conciliatory a manner as possible. Many of the former civil servants who took the oath of fidelity were retained in employment, the High Court of Justice was dissolved and a Burgher Senate of six members created, the obnoxious auction dues were repealed and a proclamation was issued declaring that, as 'the monopoly and oppression hitherto practised for the profit of the East India Company' was at an end, there was now both free trade and a free market—no new taxes to be levied, and oppressive ones to be repealed. The paper currency, which then amounted to more than a quarter of a million sterling, to hold its value, but the British to make payments in coin. All this gave great satisfaction, and no more was heard even in Swellendam about 'National Assemblies' and 'Freedom.' It was different, however, in Graaffreinet, where, under Marthinus Prinsloo, the people refused to take the oath of allegiance, and sent back the Landrost (Mr Bresler) with several absurd proposals, the answer to which was the removal of 300 men of the 84th Regiment to Stellenbosch in readiness to move forward when required, and cutting off all supplies from the rebels. However, they soon quarrelled among themselves and submitted. A party, however, was still left who cherished national principles, sent one of their number to Batavia and induced the Dutch Governor-General very foolishly to forward gunpowder and other supplies to the aid of the malcontents. The vessel in which these were sent was driven by stress of weather into Delagoa Bay, and soon afterwards captured by the British.[1] A still greater success was obtained by the new Government on the

---

[1] Subsequently Marthinus Prinsloo and A. Van Jarsveld were sentenced to death, Cornelius Edeman to be flogged and banished, while the others received lesser punishments.

17th of August 1796, when a Dutch fleet, consisting of eight ships,[1] under Rear-Admiral Lucas, surrendered almost unconditionally in Saldanha Bay.

In 1796 the British Government seemed to consider that the Cape should be retained permanently, and sent out the Earl of Macartney as Governor. It is noticeable that his salary and allowances (£12,000 per annum), together with those of half-a-dozen other officials, amounted to £20,000 per annum, whereas the total yearly revenue was scarcely £29,000. It was as the key of a position that the Cape was specially valuable, and this was now understood. So far as the Government was concerned it was pure, uncorrupt, and thoroughly identified with Conservative principles. Backed up by an overwhelming power, the inhabitants of the colony who were imbued with Jacobin principles[2] had no opportunities of asserting them. The slightest attempt at revolution

---

[1] *Revolutie* and *Dordrecht* of 66 guns each; *Admiral Tromp*, 54; *Castor*, 44; *Brave*, 40; *Bellona*, 28; *Sirene*, 26; *Hawk*, 18; *Maria*, storeship. Most of the soldiers and seamen who were taken prisoners willingly entered the British service.

[2] These prevailed extensively. On one occasion invitations were sent out by Mr Eksteen, of Bergrliet, addressed to each person as 'Citizen.' For this he had to apologise and give security to the extent of £1000 that he would not again be guilty of a similar offence.

would have been immediately repressed in the sternest manner. The new-comers were greatly disgusted with the constant system of falsehood which prevailed in connection with returns for purposes of taxation, while on the other hand there was a strong feeling among the people against the alleged arrogance and grasping character of their rulers. The burghers were made to take a new oath of allegiance at the point of the sword, and when Delport, the former 'National Commandant' of Swellendam, endeavoured to escape, he was arrested and exiled.

Mr Bresler returned to Graaffreinet as Landrost, and Mr Barrow,[1] the Governor's private secretary, accompanied him. These officers afterwards travelled eastward through the Zuuroeld, and interviewed the great chief Gaika on the banks of the Keiskamma River, with whom an agreement was made that, as a token of submission, he should periodically send to Graaffreinet one of his people, bearing a brass-headed staff with the British arms emblazoned upon it. Mr Barrow describes a mutiny which took place on board the fleet in Simons Bay, which he attributes to mere wan-

[1] Afterwards Sir John Barrow. See his most interesting *Travels in South Africa.*

tonness, declaring that sedition, like the sweating sickness in the reign of Edward IV., had become a national malady.

> 'The general air
> From pole to pole, from Atlas to the East,
> Was then at enmity with English blood.'

But Englishmen were well able to defend themselves. On board the flagship lying off the Amsterdam battery there was an open rebellion. Lord Macartney ordered the guns of the fort to be loaded, and shot to be heated in the ovens, while he despatched a message to the mutinous crew of the *Tremendous*, informing them that, if they did not hoist the Royal Standard within half an hour, as a token of unconditional surrender, he would blow their ship out of the water. Submission was made within the given time, for no one doubted that otherwise the whole battery would have been played upon her until she was destroyed.

A British vessel, named the *Star*, sent out by Commodore Alexander, took possession of the West Coast as far north as Walfish Bay, while a small piece of territory was added beyond the Tarka River, in a north-easterly direction, where our boundary was rather ill-defined. The colony now imported goods to the annual value of £253,000; slaves, £45,000; and the average exports only amounted to £15,000. Heavy military and naval expenditure provided for the difference. Lord Macartney was old, gouty, and ill-disposed to bear the enervating heat of South African summers; therefore he returned to England in 1798, and Lieutenant-General Dundas ruled in his stead.

Old Commandant Adrian Van Jarsveld having been guilty of fraud and forgery, was arrested at the Drostdy of Graaffreinet, and sent away in charge of three dragoons. Marthinus Prinsloo immediately called out the Boschberg burghers to rescue him, which they easily did. A rebellion now broke out, and Brigadier-General Vandeleur was sent to quiet it, troops being sent at the same time by sea to Algoa Bay in order to co-operate with him. These he afterwards joined, and he had the pleasure of also receiving fifty-three farmers from the Sneeuwbergen. The Dutch colonists were discouraged by the Hottentots rising against them and joining the British. The insurgents now felt compelled to lay down their arms. Ninety-three were fined, twenty became prisoners in the Capetown Castle, and a reward of £200 was offered for the capture of each of the ringleaders.

A Kafir war now broke out, in which the 81st

Regiment was attacked near the Bushmans River, and a party under Lieutenant Chumney nearly all slaughtered. Commandos were called out, but, being badly directed, did nothing. Then the Kafirs, thinking the white men were afraid to attack, devastated the eastern districts, being joined by roving bands of Hottentots. On this occasion they even crossed the Gamtoos River and ravaged a portion of the Longkloof. Nearly the whole district of Graaffreinet was in the hands of the enemy. Twenty-nine white people had lost their lives, and there was scarcely a farmhouse left standing east of the Gamtoos River. The splendid 'Laager' system saved the people. Large burgher commandos were called out, and General Dundas, with reinforcements of troops, proceeded to the frontier. A miserable peace was easily patched up when the Kafirs saw that they had nothing more to gain by war. But the colonists were disappointed and disheartened, as they knew that such a treaty was completely illusory. A stone redoubt, called Fort Frederick, was built and garrisoned at Algoa Bay, and a few dragoons and men of the Hottentot Regiment were stationed at Graaffreinet.

Missionary enterprise on an organised scale

scarcely commenced in South Africa previous to the year 1799, when the London Missionary Society sent out four agents. The Dutch East India Company's directors never seemed to consider that the conversion of the heathen was one of their responsibilities, and the colonists were almost as indifferent. We read constantly in the records of the appointment of two or three ministers as well as 'sick visitors,' and these men were, strictly speaking, as much officials of the Government as preachers of Christianity. Now an effective effort was to be made to do that which had hitherto been neglected, and to the performance of this immense work much money and great zeal, but sometimes comparatively little discretion, were applied. The biography of the first and greatest of these London missionaries is full of romance. Dr Van der Kemp began life by serving as a gallant officer in the Dutch army, and afterwards became a physician of such eminence as to hold a high position in the profession. Luxury, good society, friends, and all the refinements of civilisation were renounced that he might teach Christianity to the heathen. His eccentricities, unfortunately, militated against his usefulness. He thought it right to conform to savage customs which were not, in his opinion, sinful, and lived with a slave girl as his wife, very much in the style of the Hottentots around him. Bethelsdoop, near Port-Elizabeth, was founded by him, but never became a success. Other centres were from time to time formed, where the natives lived with a church as their centre and a pastor as director of the community. By degrees an antagonistic feeling grew up between many of the colonists and the missionaries. The latter championed the coloured races. According to their views, wars were forced on, native rights disregarded, and much injustice done. From time to time grievances were brought to the notice of the British Government, and there was always a large party at home, organised later on into the Aboriginal Protection Society, which did much harm by practically listening to only one side of the case. Of course, faults were committed on both sides. It is not reasonable to suppose that the Government and colonists were not frequently to blame, but the extremely one-sided action and opinions of men entirely wedded to a partisan view frequently impeded the march of civilisation by raising up bitter enmities. It is not possible now to pay much attention to the bitter controversies of the first half of the nineteenth century, whose numerous books, pamphlets, blue-books, dispatches and correspondence form an extensive literature.

Sir George Young, who arrived at the end of 1799 as Governor, was by no means a favourable specimen of a British official. He was so corrupt and inefficient that his removal became necessary, and General Dundas resumed the reins of Government until the transfer of the settlement to Holland. In the meantime Graaffreinet was again a centre of disaffection, and an armed force had to be sent there to keep order. Troops of Hottentots and of Kafirs infested the country, and robbed in such a manner as to force the farmers to combine against the banditti. A great commando had at last to deal with these people in the country between Algoa Bay and the Bushmans River, when no fewer than 230 savages were killed, and 13,100 head of horned cattle recovered; but, unfortunately, this success was attended with the loss of one of the bravest of the Dutch pioneers, Commandant Van der Walt, who was shot dead during an engagement with the enemy near the Baviaan's River.

By the Treaty of Amiens between France and England in 1802 it was stipulated that the possession of the Cape of Good Hope should revert to the Batavian Republic. The States-General of Holland resolved that the colony should be governed by a Governor and a Council of four members, and that the High Court of Justice should exist as an independent institution. Trade was to be unrestricted, custom's dues fixed at three per cent. on imports, no control to be exercised from Java, and British ships to be permitted to obtain supplies on the same terms as those accorded to vessels from Holland. A man of ability and excellent character was appointed Governor in the person of Lieutenant-General Janssens, and a garrison upwards of 3000 strong was sent out. In 1803 the Dutch flag again waved over the Castle of Capetown, and an opportunity was given—and was taken—of showing that Dutchmen were able to govern a colony on comparatively enlarged and enlightened principles without restrictive monopoly, and without those grasping but short-sighted methods which had done so much hitherto to damage the reputation of the Netherlands East India Company and to retard the progress of the settlement.

The first thing that the ancient owners did was to thank God publicly for the restoration of the settlement. With great industry, General Janssens visited the most distant parts of the colony, interviewed Gaika on the banks of the Fish River, and subsequently visited St Helena Bay and the Tulbagh district. The Vale of Grace (Genadendal) was established as a great Moravian mission station for Hottentots in the western districts (present Caledon division). A new military district was wisely formed in Graaffreinet, so that concerted action could be arranged against the natives. The great division of Uitenhage was declared to extend from the Kromm to the Fish River, while Tulbagh, named in honour of the beloved Governor of that name, embraced an enormous tract of country between Swellendam and the western shores of the colony washed by the South Atlantic Ocean. It was seen that a mistake had been made by introducing negro slaves, and an enlightened system of European immigration was approved of. Commissary-General De Mist, who visited the colony as an Inspector-General with full governing powers, went even further than the local authorities in projects of progress. A commission was appointed to encourage stock-breeding, agriculture and wool-farming. All religious societies were to receive equal protection from the laws, and the establishment of schools was provided for. The pernicious system of paper currency not redeemable in coin was extended, very little could be done financially, as it was difficult to obtain supplies from the almost exhausted exchequer of the Batavian Republic. Holland under republican rule was really at this time identified with France, so that when war was declared between that country and Britain, every possible effort was made to defend the Cape.

At this time there were in the settlement 25,700 people who owned more than 29,000 slaves, besides having in their service, under contract, upwards of 20,000 Hottentots. Capetown alone possessed a population of 6200 Europeans. The regular troops of all arms comprised barely 1600 men, and although every effort was made to get the inhabitants to cooperate, little was gained by constant enrolments and drilling throughout the Cape Peninsula. The blow fell at last. On the 4th of January 1806, flags from the signal station informed the authorities that a British fleet was approaching, and on the same evening no fewer than sixty-three ships of the enemy anchored between Robben Island and the Blaauwberg Strand. A gale blew during the night and made landing impossible, consequently the fleet was ordered to Saldanha Bay. Some of the ships had sailed when it was seen that the sea had gone down so much as to make landing practicable. This was consequently effected under the protection of the guns of the ships of war. Every boat safely reached the shore, with the exception of one containing thirty-five men of the 93d Regiment, all of whom were drowned.

The British army was 4000 strong, and comprised the 24th, 59th, and 83d Regiments, the Highland Brigade, a battery of artillery, as also 600 sailors, armed with pikes, and accompanied by two howitzers and six field guns. On the other hand, General Janssens had only been able to collect a motley force 2000 strong, consisting of German mercenary troops (Waldecks), burghers, crews of two French ships, Javanese artillery, Hottentot foot soldiers, and more than 100 Mozambique slaves. As this force was advancing on the morning of the 8th of January they saw the British army crossing the lower part of the Blaauwberg *en route* for Capetown. The Dutch General immediately extended his troops in line, and seemed determined to fight, although he must have well known that success was impossible. His words of encouragement were answered with cheers by all the men except those in the Waldeck battalion, who were old enough soldiers to know perfectly well that their cause was hopeless. Almost immediately after the artillery opened fire these troops began to retreat, others followed, and when the Highland Brigade advanced to charge with the bayonet, the retreat became a headlong flight so far as the main body was concerned. The French and auxiliaries behaved well, but General Janssens was forced to order them to retire. Disspirited and deserted, he saw the cause of the Batavian Republic lost in South Africa; but even at such a moment he could not but recognise the steady bravery of a small body of mounted artillery who continued to fire under the command of Lieutenant Pellegrini, who was immediately promoted on the field to the rank of captain, when the general was reluctantly obliged to command them to discontinue a hopeless contest. The recreant Waldeckers, with the exception of one company which had stood its ground, were ordered to proceed to Capetown, and Janssens then retired with a remnant of his force to the mountains of Hottentot Holland. General Baird continued his triumphant march, required possession within six hours of the Capetown military lines and

Fort Knokke, while, on application,[1] he would only grant the garrison a suspension of arms for thirty-six hours

On the 10th of January 1806, articles of capitulation were signed, and on the 11th proclamations were issued by the conqueror ordering the inhabitants to take the oath of allegiance to his Britannic Majesty, and appointing Willem Stephanus Van Ryneveld chief civil magistrate and councillor. The terms of agreement could not be considered either arbitrary or harsh. Private property was to be respected, the burghers to retain all their privileges, no soldiers to be quartered upon the inhabitants of Capetown, and the prisoners of war could proceed to Europe. Troops were at once pushed on to Stellenbosch, orders issued for a regiment to proceed to Mossel Bay, so that the Attaqua

[1] The application was for an armistice of forty-eight hours, but the stern reply was that, if within thirty-six hours the town was not surrendered, the garrison would be put to the sword. The character of Sir David Baird was stern, and an anecdote is current respecting his own mother's appreciation of it. When he was at one time taken prisoner in Egypt, and she was acquainted with the fact, her remark was, 'The Lord pity the man that's chained to our Dawvid.' During Sir David Baird's government of the Cape a man named Cornelis Maas spread a report that a French fleet had anchored in Saldanha Bay. The offender was immediately flogged round the town at a cart's tail by the public executioner, and after this no false reports were circulated.

Pass could be secured, and as it was perfectly evident that there was no chance of holding the settlement, it was formally surrendered by General Janssens on the 18th of January 1806.

On the 21st of May 1806 Du Prè Alexander, Earl of Caledon, arrived in the colony as Governor, and a pure despotism was inaugurated. The administrator personally controlled and directed every department; he was also a judge of appeal in criminal cases, could fix the prices to be paid for all military supplies, and could make what laws he pleased, completely unrestrained, even by the advice of a council. A firm rule, backed by an overwhelming force, secured complete tranquillity, broken only by a young Irish labourer and a Creole, who succeeded in plundering thirty-four farms, but were easily defeated and captured by a small military force. Fifty-one prisoners were captured and severely punished, three of their ringleaders only being put to death.

The Cape was now made a receptacle for negroes rescued by British men-of-war, and this proceeding, together with the previous practice of bringing Malay slaves from Java, laid the foundation of a class of the population which has increased so much that in Capetown alone at the present day there are are more than 12,000 of their descendants. There was little expansion in the period of British rule which preceded the year 1820. The divisions of George and Caledon were formed in 1811 and 1813 respectively, Albany and Clanwilliam in 1814, and Beaufort about the same time, but little advance of any description is noticeable. Capetown, indeed the colony, was mainly supported by lavish expenditure, civil, military and naval. So far as finance was concerned, the Cape of Good Hope was a heavy burden to any European power, which the struggling Batavian Republic could not sustain. In the country districts near the capital farmers obtained a revenue by sending in supplies to a good market, while in the remote districts a yearly visit was the most that could be made, and the population grew up unused certainly to the luxuries of civilisation, but good hunters, excellent shots, and inured to all the hardship of a pioneer settler's life. Circuit Courts were established, an ocean packet mail service commenced, special efforts were made by the establishment of a farm at Boschberg and otherwise to promote farming industries, and when a census was taken in the year 1819, the population comprised about 60,000 people, 32,000 of whom were Europeans.

Lieutenant-General Sir John Cradock was Governor from 1811 until 1813, and in the latter year Lieutenant-General Lord Charles Henry Somerset was appointed to the office. It was not until the 13th of August 1814 that the Cape Colony was formally ceded to Great Britain, along with Dutch Guiana, in consideration of a payment of £5,000,000 sterling. The settlement then was owned not merely by right of conquest, but by virtue of a commercial bargain, made with the legitimate Government of the Netherlands.

The Hottentots still remained seriously troublesome. General Janssens had recognised their division under chiefs. This was promptly repudiated by the British Government, and it was soon found that these people, desiring change and utterly unreliable, were as troublesome as they were untrustworthy. Smallpox and brandy at an early date reduced their number, but early this century great missionary efforts were made among them, reserves or locations were established for their use, and under the administration of justice, by means of Circuit Courts, many of the cases comprised charges brought by coloured people against colonists. Very serious charges were made by Mr Read of Bethelsdorp to his employers, the London Missionary Society, in 1811. According to his letter, the white people treated Hottentots with inhuman cruelty, and governors as well as landrosts were deaf to cries for humanity and justice. He asserted that in the district in which he lived (Uitenhage) more than 100 murders had been committed. The Secretary of State ordered a thorough investigation, and every facility was given to Hottentots to bring forward their grievances. The judges who prosecuted the inquiry went forth on what was styled the Black Circuit, which resulted in enormously irritating the colonists, and proving that the charges against them were so grossly exaggerated as to be virtually false. The most serious cases were decided in favour of the so-called oppressor, and about half a dozen colonists only were found guilty of crimes. The truth is that on this, as on many subsequent occasions, the missionaries were duped by men who make lying a fine art. In later days the Aborigines suffered in a similar manner, and the fashion of abusing colonists in England on *ex parte* statements has lasted continuously to the present day.

The Kafirs were much more serious enemies than the Hottentots. The latter have now succumbed to brandy drinking and other vices; the former are more numerous than ever. So far from dying out they have multiplied in such a manner as to make the question as to whether South Africa is to be eventually a white man's or a black man's country—one of those problems whose consideration we must attempt when dealing with a later period of history. Early in the century they were flushed with the memory of successful raids, and imbued with the desire not merely of plundering colonists, but of driving them out of South Africa. In 1811 the Longkloof and the western districts were seriously threatened by this savage race, marauding was constant, life was unsafe, and property insecure. The burghers of George, Swellendam, Uitenhage and Graaffreinet were called out and took the field with the Cape Regiment under the command of Colonel Graham. In spite of the large force marching against them, one of their chiefs, advancing to a party under Major Cuyler, declared, 'I *will* eat honey, and to procure it will cross the rivers Sunday, Coega and Zwartkops. The country is mine. I won it in war, and shall maintain it.' Here he admits that the Cape

Colony was owned by Hottentots, if savages can be said to own a country which they do not utilise. It thus appears that the men who ruthlessly drove them to the westward were the people whom we in turn conquered. The fierce denunciation of colonists for stripping Kafirs of their right, and taking their country from them, is one of those injustices which long animated European policy, and considerably tended to alienate people whom it would have been wise to conciliate. On the occasion of the war to which we are now referring, upwards of 2000 white men took the field, 1200 of whom were soldiers, and these included a large Hottentot contingent. Proceedings opened by mistaken generosity on the one side, and savage treachery on the other. Landrost Stockenstrom, acting in direct opposition to orders, but animated by a philanthropic motive, advanced with twenty-four men to parley with the enemy, and, if possible, persuade the fierce Kafirs to lay down their arms. A friendly parley went on for about half an hour, but then there was a rush from all sides, and the Landrost, his interpreter, and eight farmers were immediately stabbed to death. Prompt retribution visited the murderers, as the Landrost's son, Ensign Stockenstrom, pursued them with a small force, and killed sixteen of their number. Various engagements followed. In a few months afterwards the Kafirs were driven across the Fish River and the war ended, while a line of military posts was established to defend the frontier.

# CHAPTER VI.

Sir John Cradock—Kafir War and Battle of Grahamstown—The Rebellion and Trial of Bezuidenhout—Grievances of Dutch Colonists—The Settlers of 1820—The Poet Pringle and Liberty of the Press—Inflated Currency and Government Expenditure—Colonel Smith—Another Kafir War—Death of Hintza—Slave Emancipation—Sir George Napier—The War of the Axe—The Emigrant Boers—Christmas Day, 1850—Another Kafir War—Sir George Cathcart—Expansion of the Colony—Representative Institutions.

GENERAL SIR JOHN CRADOCK was obliged to investigate thoroughly into allegations made in England respecting the cruel conduct of frontier farmers to aboriginal natives, and His Excellency, at the conclusion of his labours, emphatically declares that he 'approves of the good and unoffending conduct of the inhabitants of the frontier towards the Kafir tribes, the faithless and unrelenting disturbers of the peace and prosperity of this colony.' This procedure has been continued at intervals ever since. There have always been three parties—the natives, their philanthropic friends in Europe, and the colonists. The last are generally condemned on *prima facie* evidence, and the savages are credited with qualities which betray thorough ignorance of their character. Of course, colonists have been sometimes blameworthy; but the terrible mistake has been generally made of condemning them unheard, and on insufficient evidence. Wars with the natives in South Africa were recurrent, and persistent Kafir robberies always provoked them.

Again the curtain rose on a tragedy, when colonial troops were sent in 1818 to the assistance of the paramount chief Gaika, who had been conquered by men of his own household. Colonel Brereton crossed the Fish River, and, having Gaika's people as auxiliaries, signally defeated the enemy. Makana[1] was the

[1] 'Makana's Gathering,' or War Song, by Pringle, commences:—

>Wake! Amakosa, wake!
>  And arm yourselves for war,
>As coming winds the forests shake,
>  I hear a sound from far.
>It is not thunder in the sky,
>  Nor lion's roar upon the hill,
>But the voice of Him who sits on high,
>  And bids me speak His will.
>
>He bids me call you forth,
>  Bold sons of Rarabe,
>To sweep the white man from the earth,
>  And drive them to the sea;
>The sea which heaved them up at first,
>  For Amakosa's curse and bane
>Howls for the progeny she nurst,
>  To swallow them again.

moving spirit against the British, and it was he who denounced the wrath of the spirits against those who should hold aloof from the contest. He organised an attack upon the newly-established military station at Grahamstown, which gave an opportunity for a heroic and successful defence to a garrison of 223 men, whose exertions did in that day for the Cape Colony what in our own times was performed at Rorke's Drift for Natal. From the hills commanding the devoted fort, streams of barbarians, full of ferocity and strength, descended like a torrent on the small band of soldiers drawn up to receive them; but when they were only a few paces distant, a terrific hail of musketry poured into them which flesh and blood were unable to withstand. Another army of Kafirs was led against the barracks by Makana in person, who gave orders for the use of shortened assegais in a hand-to-hand combat. But a deadly fire from the protected positions of the barrack square also turned this stream back to its source. The other columns rallied and returned to the attack only to be again discomfited. Grahamstown and the eastern districts of the colony were saved. The invasion of Kafirland subsequently took place when our columns took possession of the natural native bush fortresses of the Fish River, captured 30,000 cattle, and broke the power of Ndlambe, the enemy of Gaika and of his British allies. The Keiskamma River was now made the eastern boundary of the colony.

The people of Dutch extraction specially resented the representations made by missionaries and others against them and their fellow-colonists. Increased taxation further aggravated discontent, and neither the Government nor the administration of the law was loved or respected. As fully illustrative of a spirit which greatly tended to the exodus which so materially helped forward the expansion of Southern Africa, the celebrated case of Bezuidenhout is most instructive. This man refused to appear before a deputy landrost when charged with ill-treating a coloured servant. The case was then taken to the Circuit Court at Graaffreinet, and the judges ordered his arrest; Hottentot soldiers were employed to perform this duty under a European officer, and Bezuidenhout took refuge in a cave and fired upon them. There he was shot, and when his relatives and friends came to the funeral they declared beside the open grave that they would be revenged. An effort even was made to obtain assistance from the Kafir chief Gaika, and all the Dutch farmers were called upon to rally round the standard of revolution raised at Slagters Nek. A few obeyed the call, but these had soon to lay down their arms to a party of dragoons and burghers. On the 9th of March 1816 six ringleaders were executed, and a feeling of enmity and dissatisfaction found expression in subsequent years, when Boers, dissatisfied with the British Government, called upon each other to remember 'Slagters Nek.'

The great distress which prevailed in England after the battle of Waterloo turned the attention of Government to the necessity of encouraging emigration, and in 1819 the British House of Commons voted £50,000 to send families to South Africa. Ninety thousand applications were received, and out of these about 5000 emigrants were chosen who landed in Algoa Bay in 1820, formed the settlement of Albany, and became the nucleus of a European population in the Eastern districts of the Cape Colony, which has repaid the mother country a hundredfold by developing the resources of a country whose chief trade, computed now by many millions pounds sterling per annum, is carried on with the mother country. The bread cast upon the waters returned, as the men and women sent out in 1820 were indomitable settlers whom no disasters terrified nor disappointments turned back. Droughts, locusts, floods, rust in wheat, are to be enumerated among the enemies to their progress; but, above all, they and their children suffered from Kafir wars, which utterly devastated the country and ruined the farmers. Nevertheless, they persevered, and now the eastern districts of the Cape Colony have become as peaceable and secure as the county of Surrey. Sheep farming and ostrich farming are successfully prosecuted, while among the foremost men at the great mineral centres of South Africa, now attracting the attention of the world, we can specially call attention to sons of the British settlers of 1820.

Certainly there has been an enormous expansion of liberty in South Africa since the days of Lord Charles Somerset. When Mr Thomas Pringle, the poet, asked permission in 1823 to publish a monthly magazine, the Governor thought it his duty to forward the prospectus to the Home Government, and was informed in reply that in the proposed publication no topics of personal or political controversy could be referred to. In the prospectus of *The South African Commercial Advertiser* there was an abject servility which at once met with the favourable approval of the authorities. This journal 'would ever most rigidly exclude all personal controversy, however disguised, or the remotest discussion of subjects relating to the policy or administration of the Colonial Government.' Lord Charles Somerset approved, but a little later Thomas Pringle and John Fairbairn became joint editors of this newspaper. Their free expression of opinion soon gave such offence that the printing press was seized and the issue of their journal prohibited. Earl Bathurst, then Secretary of State, was appealed to, and some concessions were made, but the autocratic Governor could not dominate the independent spirit of the great South African poet. Pringle resigned his office as librarian, and declined to conduct a paper under the fetters and restrictions which it was desired to impose upon him. Lord Charles Somerset was subsequently ordered to England, that he might furnish explanations with regard to a host of charges made against him—most of which were exaggerated or false—but never after this time was the liberty of the press infringed within South Africa.

In 1825 the bubble of an inflated currency, not redeemable in gold, had to be dissipated, and to effect this object each rixdollar was made equivalent in value to one shilling and sixpence. Coin to the amount of £56,000 was sent from England, and there was an end of Goverment issue of notes. The milch cow of the colonists was the Government expenditure in Capetown and Simons Town. Subsequently this was supplemented by officers of the Indian service making the Cape Colony a health sanatorium in which they spent the leisure obtained by leave of absence. Farming progress was slow, and it was a long period before, in the eastern districts, woolled sheep received attention. At a later period the value of the magnificent sheep walks of the Karoo was fully recognised, while much nearer our own period the silver fleece of the angora goat, as well as ostrich feathers, were added to the exports of the colony.

In early days there was great poverty and a terrible struggle. To detail these, as well as to speak of the manner in which they were surmounted, would certainly lead us to admire qualities of patience, bravery and perseverance, without which it is impossible to build up a nation. In the west improvements were chiefly confined to Capetown, where a library and various useful institutions were founded, and mercantile enterprise kept progress with Government expenditure.

The establishment of a Supreme Court under royal charter, the abolition of the Boards of Landrost and Heemraden, with the substitution of Civil Commissioners, the formation of several new divisions, and an improved system of Government under such men as Sir Rufane Shawe Donkin, who founded Port Elizabeth, Sir G. Lowry Cole and Sir Benjamin D'Urban, helped forward the slow progress of the Cape Colony. Commissioners had been sent from England to South Africa as well as to all the principal British settlements, and these men spent years in collecting materials for extensive reports, but the Home Secretary and the British members of the House of Commons seemed persistently to avoid a competent acquaintance with the wants and requirements of the country. Up to a very recent period the study of the geography and history of ancient Greece seemed to be considered more useful and desirable than a knowledge of the course of events and statistics of those dependencies on which the commerce, and therefore the prosperity, of the Empire principally depend. Port Elizabeth became by degrees the prosperous port of the eastern districts of the Cape Colony, because of the expansion of agricultural and pastoral industries, consequent upon the advent of British settlers in 1820. Dairy industries so flourished that 'Algoa Bay' butter became an article of export, and this was followed by success both in cattle and sheep breeding. Kafir wars, however, broke out periodically, and the history of the new portion of the settlement is, for more than fifty years, a narrative of a struggle with fierce barbarians.

The first great war broke out in 1834, when the Hottentots of the Kat River Missions allied themselves with the Kafirs. From the beautiful valleys of Bathurst the cattle of the poor struggling settlers was carried off on Christmas Day. Homesteads, herds, flocks, the accumulations of hard labour and industry for many years, had to be abandoned, and shelter sought in Grahamstown. In one or two places the farmers boldly and successfully stood their ground, but the surprise was great, preparation was wanting, and the country was, therefore, pillaged and laid waste. Hundreds of fugitives, leaving everything they possessed in the world, hurried to places of comparative safety. Bravery and resolution were, however, sometimes successful, as when near the Kat River, thirty men, when impetuously attacked by 150 Kafirs, fired with such steadiness and effect as to rout the enemy. Hermanus Kraal, eighteen miles from Grahamestown, defended by a small detachment of the 75th Regiment, was attacked in vain, and on the evening of that day the future hero of Aliwal—Colonel Smith—concluded an historic ride of six days from Capetown to the frontier. Martial law was proclaimed, volunteers called out, and the enemy attacked in their own strongholds. The arrival of Sir Benjamin d'Urban and of the 72nd Regiment filled the colonists with hope, although this Governor was so impressed with the lamentable state of affairs then existing, that he declared that the land was filled with the lamentations of the widows and the fatherless, and that the indelible impressions made upon his mind by this irruption of savages were such, as to make him regard as trifles all he had previously seen in a military career of thirty years.

Colonel Smith directed the forces with energy and ability. The great bushy fastnesses of the Fish River were cleared, and a forward and successful progress was made across the Keiskamma, followed by a general movement upon the Amatolas, under the direction of Sir Benjamin d'Urban, who had assumed the chief command. The Fingoes now joined the British forces, and Hintza, the paramount Kafir chief, was so seriously pressed as to sue for peace. He was taken as a hostage and informed that he would be shot if he made any attempt to escape. Nevertheless, this wily chieftain, thinking he had a chance of joining his people, suddenly, when under escort, put spurs to his horse and endeavoured to escape. An exciting scene then occurred. Colonel Smith pursued him at full gallop, and after having snapped his pistols and hurled them at Hintza's head, he made a tremendous exertion, by means of which he got alongside the fugitive, and flung himself furiously upon him. Both fell to the ground, but Hintza managed to extricate himself and hurled an assegai at his adversary. Several men of the Corps of Guides now came upon the scene, but Hintza, deaf to their calls, although wounded, rushed down hill in order to gain the shelter of a neighbouring thicket. Southey, one of the guides, during the pursuit, saw an assegai strike a rock upon which he was climbing, and turning suddenly round, beheld Hintza close at hand in the act of throwing an assegai at him. In an instant his gun was fired, and the moment after the great paramount chief of Kafirland ceased to live. The British troops then pushed forward to the Umtata River. The Fingoe nation, about 17,000 in number, and with 22,000 cattle, entered the colony under British protection; the province of Queen Adelaide, between the Keiskamma and Kei Rivers, was added to the colony; King William's Town, on the Buffalo, was established, and peace was proclaimed to exist between Kreli, the son of Hintza, and the British nation.

Her Majesty's Government viewed the proceedings of the war with disapprobation. Lord Glenelg, the Colonial Secretary, did not hesitate to state in an official despatch that the conduct of the colonists and of the local authorities fully justified the Kafirs in going to war, and consequently commanded the claim of sovereignty just acquired by hard fighting over the newly-conquered province should be at once renounced. Captain Stockenstrom was shortly afterwards appointed Lieutenant-Governor of the eastern districts, and specially charged with carrying out this decree, which was naturally most distasteful to the loyal English settlers, and tended still further to alienate the people of Dutch extraction. Utterly foolish and unjust though it was, and probably the cause of subsequent Kafir wars, it had, nevertheless, a wonderful effect upon the expansion of Southern Africa, as when Pieter Retief remonstrated with indignation and without effect, 6000 people of his own nationality followed him into the interior, determined at all risks to find a home where they could live without fear of taxes, unjust government, and the ignorant or malicious interference of distant rulers. There were other reasons. Slaves had been emancipated by Great Britain, and inadequate compensation, reduced much by passing through the hands of agents, had been doled out to the owners; vagrancy was practically unrestrained; unjustifiable odium had been cast upon the inhabitants by missionary reports readily believed in England; so when the culminating and surprising stroke fell from the hand of Lord Glenelg, the cup of wrath and indignation was full to the brim, and the unknown wilds became far preferable to the Cape Colony. The Voortrekkers went forth, and the deeds which we shall soon refer to have been the powerful means of opening up to civilisation most of that vast territory which will yet form one of the greatest confederation of states in the southern hemisphere.

## Expansion of Southern Africa    117

As was inevitable from the policy pursued, the frontier again became unquiet in 1840, and Governor Sir George Napier was forced to proceed there and hold a grand 'palaver' with the Kafir chiefs. However, it was not until the beginning of 1846 that Sandilli joined a war party, and soon found a pretext for hostilities in the apprehension of a Kafir for stealing a hatchet, which gave rise to the 'war of the axe.' When this prisoner was on his way to Grahamstown, he was rescued by the wrist of the Hottentot to whom he was manacled being severed to set him free. For two years an expensive, irritating and disastrous war raged. An insufficient force was, in the first instance, sent against the enemy. At Burnshill mission station there was a disaster; Fort Victoria was abandoned, and 4000 cattle were captured from us at Peddie. The burghers of Colesberg Cradock and Graaffreinet had to take the field to stem a tide of invasion, which was not effectually turned until at the battle of Gwanga, near the Keiskamma River, the 7th Dragoon Guards, with the Cape Corps and other troops, succeeded in surprising 600 Kafir warriors, who showed a bold front at first, but were soon broken and trampled down. The Fingoe levies finished what the cavalry had commenced, and ferociously searching for their hereditary enemies among the long grass, despatched them without hesitation or mercy. A large force was afterwards sent to the Amatolas, and subsequently crossed the Kei. Nevertheless, the Kafirs continued the contest, and it was found necessary to send out Sir Harry Smith, who had added Indian laurels to those previously won by him in South Africa. The Keiskamma was now made the colonial boundary, and British Kaffraria formed. No further operations were, however, then necessary, as a great meeting was held in King William's Town, when Sandilli, with the other chiefs, agreed to the proposals of Government, and what was called peace resulted. Then the new Governor declared the northern border of the country to be the Orange River, and a new division between it and the Stormbergen was constituted, under the name of Albert.

There was no real peace in South Africa. The Kafirs had only consented to a truce in which they could recruit their strength for renewed depredations, and those inhabitants of Dutch extraction who had endeavoured to find a new home in the interior were surprised and indignant when the British rule, which they had done so much to escape, was proclaimed in the new territory which they considered to be their own.  Under Pretorius, the emigrant Boers declared their complete independence, but the country styled the Sovereignty was relentlessly claimed, the Boers' claim to liberty was styled a revolt, and £1000 reward was offered for the capture of their leader.  Sir Harry Smith crossed the Orange River, and not far from that stream, in the present Orange Free State, on the 19th of July 1848, was fought the battle of Boomplaats, where the Boers were defeated, and sorrowfully compelled to trek beyond the Vaal River, and there to found the South African Republic.  Expansion in this way was forced on, while in the colony on the eastern frontier, the settlers had soon again to fight for the retention of their farms and the safety and lives of themselves and their families. The terrible Christmas Day of 1850 will never be forgotten.  On that special day of peace on earth and goodwill to man, the Kafirs relentlessly rushed upon defenceless villagers, and slaughtered the inhabitants.  In one place the settlers were assembled in the street listening to news brought by three Cape Corps men, when a whistle was given as a signal, and the Kafirs, rushing in, killed ten or fifteen unarmed men. The others fled to a dismantled clay building, and there took refuge with defenceless women and children. Twenty-eight men were butchered there, in the presence of females, distracted with the frightful spectacle. To show the real character of the 'noble' savage, illustrative incidents are useful. One woman who escaped said that it was customary for the Kafirs to visit at Christmas, and as usual they came, and as usual received a good dinner. They enjoyed themselves, partook freely of the good things provided, and then on a given signal murdered their hospitable entertainers. The Governor (Sir H. Smith) was shut up in Fort Cox and nearly captured. The Hottentots joined the Kafirs, a panic took place throughout the frontier districts, several forts were attacked, of which one was captured, and the war became the most serious that had yet been waged in South Africa. The burghers were called out, special contingents enrolled, and although our Hottentot *protégés* betrayed us, the Fingoes we had saved from captivity remained our staunch friends. The Kafirs absolutely overran all the Somerset, Lower Albany and Alexandria districts, and then we had to fight against a desperate foe in the dangerous woody defiles of the Amatola Mountains. The gallant Colonel Fordyce was killed in clearing the Waterkloof, but extensive operations against Kreli resulted in his defeat, and the capture of 20,000 head of cattle.

Among the disasters of the time must be commemorated the ever memorable incident, when more than 400 men, including soldiers of the 74th Highlanders and a large number of British sailors, drew up in line on the deck of the *Birkenhead*, and, allowing the women and children to be saved in the boats, went down with the ship. Danger Point in the Southern Atlantic is a natural rocky monument, which points out for ever the place where these heroes died.

The Kafir war was so protracted and expensive, that an experienced and able officer, who afterwards died for his country in the Crimea, was sent out as Governor and Commander-in-chief. Sir George Cathcart acted with vigour, and crossing the Kei, swept Kreli's country with columns of troops, burghers and levies. A force of 2000 men was sent across the Orange River to punish Moshesh, one of the allied chieftains, but, unfortunately, at the battle of Berea it is impossible to say that we obtained a victory.

However, this wily leader only used the occasion to make a favourable treaty of peace.

The ferocity and daring of the Kafirs was now changed to mere passive resistance, and peace was declared early in the year 1853. Sir George Cathcart was wise enough to see that the real bulwark of defence against savages was an adequate number of reliable white men. Consequently, the Queenstown division was formed, and its lands parcelled out to stalwart champions of order. The settlers had by this time increased and multiplied. As among the ancient Persians, so among the inhabitants of the frontier, to ride and shoot were essential qualifications, and it was soon discovered by the natives that the white inhabitants alone were sufficient to protect the country.

By degrees, during the first half of the century, considerable improvements were effected. Courts of Justice were established, the colony was divided into two parts, and a lieutenant-governor given to the eastern districts; missionary institutions were formed, in which, at such places as Kat River and Genadendal, the Hottentots received special attention; slavery was abolished, and moderate compensation given to owners of slaves; good roads were made and passes formed through those chains of mountains which divide the coast from the interior. The mass of the inhabitants, however, never felt contented. The grievances of the people of Dutch extraction, from whom the Voortrekkers sprung, was the principal cause of the expansion of the entire country. They took their grievances with them into the wilds of Southern Africa, where great and prosperous states now exist. Those who remained in the colony in doubt, prompted by the English settlers, soon began to agitate for more liberty than that accorded by autocratic military governors and the ill-informed and prejudiced rule of Downing Street. A spirit of independence showed itself in the exertions which terminated in securing a press free from the trammels of official dictation; and when, in 1848, an order in Council was issued by the Queen empowering the Secretary of State to send convicts to the Cape of Good Hope, great indignation was expressed by all classes; crowded public meetings condemned this policy as destructive of colonial interests, and the people leagued together neither to employ nor shelter felons, and to hold no intercourse with those who did. Boycotting was applied effectually long before the word was invented; and when the transport *Neptune* arrived with convicts in September 1849, the new-comers and every civil and military officer of the Crown were threatened with starvation. Under all the circumstances, the Governor, Sir Harry Smith, thought it wise not to use force, and no great interval elapsed before a note came from the British minister stating that the plan of making the Cape a penal settlement had been abandoned.

A nominee council long assisted the Governor, but at last the frequently-expressed wishes of colonists were heard, and on the 21st of April 1853, despatches were received conveying orders of the Privy Council approving of the 'Ordinances passed in the Colony constituting a Parliament for the Cape of Good Hope, consisting of a Legislative Council and a House of Assembly elected under a very wide and liberal system of franchise.' Representative government was then inaugurated in the Cape Colony, to be supplemented by responsible government in 1872.

## CHAPTER VII

Brief Sketch of Natal History—The Voortrekkers—The
Zulus—The Orange River—Sovereignty.

IN the first decade of Barros,[1] we read that in 1497 the small fleet of Vasco da Gama continued tormented by strong currents until, on the day of the Nativity of our Lord, they passed by the coast of Natal, to which they gave that name. Until the nineteenth century this fertile and beautiful portion of South Africa has no history. During the occupation of the Cape by the Dutch East India Company, occasional visits were paid to it, and a few unfortunate mariners were shipwrecked on its shores. The Dutch East India Company asserted a right to the country because of a purchase from a native chief. A 'factory' even

[1] Describing the voyage of Vasco da Gama made with four ships for the discovery of the Indies. The edition quoted in the *Annals of Natal* is that published in the *Renowned Voyages of the Portuguese to India*, dedicated to Mr Abraham Van Riebeck, Governor-General of the Netherlands, and published at Amsterdam in 1727.

was commenced, but shortly afterwards abandoned. The Zulu nation were masters of the east coast from the Umzumvooboo to Delagoa Bay up to a comparatively recent period. In 1824 the native rulers received Europeans with friendship, and a body of Zulus under the control of Englishmen collected at the Port (Natal). Forty persons arrived from Capetown, and a very little settlement was formed under the terrible shadow of Chaka's protection, whose people, when they first saw white men, supposed them 'to be of the brute species in the form only of man, and whose language was as unintelligible as the chatter of baboons.' The first Englishmen in Natal were greatly impressed by the Zulu power. Two Europeans who went to visit Chaka were surrounded by 12,000 men in their war attire, and the proud monarch declared that he was the greatest king in existence. His people were as innumerable as the stars, and his cattle uncountable. He was certainly the most powerful ruler in South-Eastern Africa, and during the eight years of his reign, conquered and laid waste the whole country between the Amapondas and the southern and most western parts of De la Goa. But Nemesis was at hand. Chaka dreamt that he was dead, and that the people served another king, and foolishly told his dream, which was looked upon as a portent, and induced Dingaan to lie in wait, stab his brother to death, and seize upon the kingdom.

The Voortrekkers reached Natal in 1837, and sent a deputation to wait upon the new Zulu king. The main body of the emigrants was left behind at a distance of five days' journey from the capital, while Mr Retief, their delegate, with sixty men, advanced. Dingaan consented to allow them to settle in a territory 400 miles in extent. The agreement was to be signed without delay, and there was no suspicion of treachery. With great diplomacy and cunning the fears of the small but intrepid band of Dutchmen were soothed to rest. They slept outside the town, and were induced to leave their guns behind, when early in the morning they were invited to visit Dingaan, conclude their business, and say farewell. They were received with effusive kindness, and offered refreshments. While they were unsuspectingly enjoying his hospitality, Dingaan issued the fatal order to his young soldiers, who easily overpowered the few unarmed emigrants, and having put them to death, bore their bodies off to a hill, on which criminals were executed, and where their corpses lay to be feasted upon by flocks of vultures hovering over the place. This dreadful deed was quickly followed by a night attack of the Zulu army upon the main camp of the emigrants, distant about five days' journey. The surprise was partially successful, but the savages were repulsed from the main camp, and next day a detachment of the emigrants followed the enemy, and recovered from them a portion of the sheep which they had carried off. It was now evident that the cruel Zulu power must be crushed, or the white man could not live in South-Eastern Africa. The Voortrekkers, inured to hardships, smarting under the lash of treachery, and bitterly resentful of the disaster they had encountered, and the lives which had been lost, now concentrated all their forces, and were joined by a few Europeans and Hottentots. One thousand three hundred determined men, with arms of precision, were now to try their strength against the most successful and warlike nation of Southern Africa. At Blood River on Sunday, the 16th of December 1838, the Zulus attacked the emigrants under Pretorius in their cantonments at five in the morning. The battle lasted for five and a half hours, and then the natives fled, and were pursued until sunset. No fewer than 3600 Zulus were slaughtered, while of the Boers none were killed, and only two wounded. Three days afterwards the King's kraal was taken, where the cruel murder of the envoys had taken place, and the bodies of these men were found uninjured. Two hundred and sixty men were now sent out by Pretorius, in order that this great success might be followed up, but having captured spies of the enemy's, they believed their falsehood, and were led into an ambuscade, and with difficulty succeeded in fighting their way through thousands of Zulus, who surrounded them. Subsequently 7000 head of cattle were captured, and the entire victorious force returned to the country occupied by the emigrants between the Little Tugela and Bushmans Rivers.

Panda treacherously intrigued against his brother Dingaan, and entered into an alliance with the emigrants, who, watching him closely, called upon him and his followers to commence the fight on the occasion of the next battle. He did so, and, his forces were beginning to waver when the effective long guns of the farmers were directed at the enemy, and caused them to waver, break their ranks, and flee. The Boers pursued and slaughtered their enemies, while Dingaan retired to mountain fastnesses, where he was killed, and Panda thus became king of the Zulus, under the surveillance and control of the emigrants, who now occupied the colony of Natal as their own, founded Pietermaritzburg, made D'Urban their port, and by a general election of the people, established a Volksraad or Parliament at the former town. Stephanus Maritz was the first president in 1839, and the descendants of the Dutch, forced from their homes in the Cape Colony, found fresh fields and pastures new among the beautiful hills and valleys of what has been subsequently styled the garden colony of South Africa. Previous to the conclusion of hostilities they captured no fewer than 40,000 cattle from their savage enemy, and soon found themselves in a prosperous and safe position. Their exodus had led them into a fair land of promise out of the British house of bondage.[1]

[1] The facts in the text are taken from the interesting narrative of Willem Jurgen Pretorius, who might truly say of the events he chronicles, *magna pars fui*. This account is given in the text of *The Annals of Natal*, by John Bird, which contain, in a rough and unhewn shape, the materials in full of a complete history of Natal. Very interesting lectures on 'The Voortrekkers of South Africa' were delivered before the Literary Society of Pretoria by the Hon. John Tudhope. The following is an extract bearing reference to the action of the Boers after the slaughter of their people by Dingaan :—' When Pieter Uys heard of the disaster which had befallen his friends, he at

In 1834 the merchants of Capetown petitioned the King in council to take measures for the occupation of Port Natal, but Sir Benjamin D'Urban said that such a settlement would

once crossed the Berg to their assistance. Thus reinforced, a command of 350 men proceeded against Dingaan. It was a bold and masterly stroke, showing the stubborn spirit of the men "cast down but not in despair." Heavily as they had suffered, they saw it was necessary to show Dingaan that they were still able to hold their own, and would punish him for his treachery. Pieter Lowras Uys and Hendrik Potgieter were the joint leaders of the force, and with Uys was his son Dirk Cornelis, a lad of fourteen. The commander saw nothing of the enemy until within a mile or two of the great place. There the Zulu army awaited them. Without hesitation Uys and his men attacked them. Riding swiftly up within twenty yards of one large division, he delivered a destructive fire, and in a short time the Zulus were in full retreat. In pursuing them the farmers got separated into small parties, and were led into an ambush, whence they had to fight their way out with a loss of ten of their number, among whom were Pieter Uys—the brave, the chivalrous Uys—and his gallant son. The manner of his death was most touching, and will remain for all time an example of filial devotion, only equalled by that of the boy in "Casabianca," commemorated by Mrs Hemans's well-known poem. While assisting a wounded comrade out of danger, Uys received a mortal wound, and called out to his men to leave them, and save themselves. Slowly and reluctantly Dirk turned to obey, but had only proceeded a few yards, when, looking round, he saw a powerful Zulu in the act of stabbing his father. Rushing back he shot the Zulu and another of the enemy, and then fell, pierced with wounds, on his father's body. "Lovely and pleasant in their lives, in death they were not divided." Englishmen will not forget that forty-one years afterwards, under somewhat similar circumstances, the brother of the little hero lost his life at the Hlobane mountain fighting under Sir Evelyn Wood against the same ruthless foe.'

require probably a force of not less than 100 men for its protection, and that these could not conveniently be taken from the troops in the Cape Colony. When a captain in the Royal Navy was appointed magistrate in 1837, the few inhabitants at D'Urban protested, and declared that 'this country of Natal is not an acknowledged part of the British dominions, but a free settlement.' After the defeat and death of Dingaan, the whole country became a Boer republic, so loosely governed, that when a landrost ordered a farmer to return some head of cattle which he had illegally withheld from a Hottentot, the farmer openly declared that he would shoot the first messenger or other functionary who should come on his premises. No one therefore dared to execute the warrant.[1]

Downing Street became alarmed by the exodus of 500 farmers from the eastern districts of the Cape Colony. According to this distant and rather partially informed authority, the emigrants 'had carried off by fraud or violence a number of individuals, formerly

---

[1] This case came under the personal observation of Mr Commissioner Cloete, afterwards Judge Cloete, and is referred to in his Lectures. See also *Bird's Annals of Natal*, Vol. I. p. 388. For information regarding early Natal events, specially with reference to Boer migrations, there is a vast amount of reliable information in *The History of the Boers in South Africa*, by Theal, London : Swan, Sonnenschein & Co.

their slaves and lately their apprenticed labourers.' 'The enormities committed by them in-
' duced Her Majesty's Government to discoun-
' tenance and punish by all lawful means the
' acts of aggression and plunder which it was
' too much the practice of these emigrants to
' perpetrate.' Sir George Napier's despatch to
Lord Glenelg, dated 18th May 1838, recommends the military occupation of Port Natal in order to protect the natives of that part of South Africa from extermination or slavery by the Boers; and as the British inhabitants had dared to help the emigrants against the Zulus, and thus throw off their allegiance, 'it was necessary to vindicate the character of the British nation.' Accordingly, towards the close of 1838, a small force of 100 men was sent to Natal. Subsequently, disturbances took place between the emigrants and the Pondos, and Sir George Napier was convinced that the interests he represented were jeopardised. In his hands he held full power for the military reoccupation of the country, and accordingly sent off a force to check the Boers in Pondoland. His Excellency informed the Volksraad at Pietermaritzburg that Her Majesty would not recognise the emigrants as an independent people, and that, so far

from allowing them to form a free State, he would lose no time in reoccupying the country.

This was terrible news to men who had struggled and bled for freedom. Joachim Prinsloo and eighteen of the members of the little Parliament of the newly-formed State declared that they knew that there was a God who is the ruler of heaven and earth, and who has power and is willing to protect the injured, though weaker, against oppressors. In Him they put their trust. 'Fate seems therefore to drive us to one of two choices, namely, to bend ourselves like oxen to bear willingly the burden imposed upon us until, finding it too heavy, we commence as before a new emigration,' or, in defence, to take arms, and 'with our fall or failure, end our troubles upon earth.' The little British force ordered to proceed from Pondoland to Natal consisted of only 263 men, mostly of the 27th Regiment, with one howitzer and two light field pieces, which, on arrival at their destination, encamped on a plain at the base of the Berea hill, about half a mile from the few buildings which formed the embryo town of D'Urban. Burghers were now called out, and Captain Smith was ordered to leave the country, but, in reply, merely said that he intended to stay. An unfortunate sortie was made, but repulsed, and now the little garrison saw itself cooped up in danger of either being starved to death or of the fort being stormed by an irresistible force. Hundreds of miles of wild country, intersected by deep rivers, intervened between them and reinforcements, but, as the danger was great, so was the opportunity. Richard King, whose name should ever live in South African history, bravely undertook to ride to the headquarters of the troops in Grahamstown, and his heroism can be estimated by some knowledge of the immense difficulties and dangers of his journey. Ferried across the lagoon, so as to avoid passing the farmers' camp, he had to ride through countries peopled by savages, swimming large rivers, camping under the canopy of heaven, obtaining food where he could snatch a meal, braving the cupidity of many and the treachery of all. He safely passed through the territories of the Pondos and the Kafirs, reached the Fish River, and arrived in the same town which was afterwards the terminal point of the famous ride of Sir Harry Smith from Capetown.

At Grahamstown, there was no delay in

despatching reinforcements, but, in the meantime, the little British garrison was in sore straits. The camp was invested, and fire opened upon it from an eighteen-pounder and two six-pounders, which had been captured. Captain Smith, however, determined to fight to the very last, although 600 men, with artillery, were opposed to him. A little vessel named the *Mazeppa* managed to sail out under a heavy fire to look for a British man-of-war, and on her fruitless return from Delagoa Bay, found the frigate *Southampton* at anchor. Richard King's ride had borne fruit, and reinforcements had arrived from the Cape Colony. A wing of the 25th Regiment, with other troops, were landed, the siege was raised, and the brave men who held the fort relieved, while the farmers, seeing that resistance was impossible, went back to their farms, and in spite of an absurd pretence that the country was under the protection of the Netherlands, the inevitable had to be accepted, and Natal became a British possession.

On the 12th of May 1843, Sir George Napier issued a proclamation appointing Advocate Henry Cloete Her Majesty's Commissioner for Port Natal, and announcing that this district, 'according to such convenient limits as should be fixed' upon and defined, would be adopted as a British colony. Mr Cloete had not only to meet 600 discontented farmers at Pietermaritzburg, but he was induced to attend a mass meeting of the women, from which he was not allowed to retire until he had listened for two hours to a violent harangue delivered by the Dutch reformed minister's wife. What a subject for a historical painting—the British Commissioner reluctantly held captive by a woman, while he was told that rather than again submit to English rule, the farmers and their wives would march barefoot over the mountains to liberty or death. Submission, of course, was a necessity, followed by another exodus which strengthened the future South African Republic.[1] But it did not merely do that. It filled an extensive and valuable portion of South Africa with a race of people who treasured an hereditary hatred to that Power which, from their point of view, had in turn exiled them from the Cape and from Natal.

On the 31st of May 1844, Natal was officially declared to be a portion of the Cape Colony; but it soon drifted under a separate Lieutenant-

---

[1] How well subsequently were the words of the Psalmist exemplified: 'As arrows in the hand of the mighty, so are the children of those cast out.'

Governor, with a separate existence of its own. On the 13th of November 1845, Mr Martin West was sent from Grahamstown, where he had been civil commissioner of Albany, to administer the affairs of the new colony, assisted by an executive council comprising the principal officers of the Government. A number of emigrant farmers desired if possible to remain under the British flag, but found the task impossible. After the establishment of the Colonial Government, actual occupation of land for one year previous to the arrival of Commissioner Cloete had to be proved in order to obtain title, and this was an impossible task. Pretorius, the leader of the Boers, abandoned his own farm close to Pietermaritzburg, and was chosen, together with another delegate, to lay the farmers' grievances before Governor Sir Henry Pottinger in Grahamstown; but although they repeatedly tried to obtain an interview, His Excellency declined to see them. Pretorius appealed to the colonial press, and specially referred to two cases in which Zulus had been unjustly preferred to himself. All was in vain. The people whose representatives were thus treated considered themselves as Israelites under the oppressive sway of Pharaoh. Death in the desert was preferable to a life of slavery, so, throwing off the dust of Natal from their feet, a great stream of refugees flowed over the Vaal River into the country which has now become the El Dorado of South Africa.

On the 8th of March 1848, Sir Harry Smith proclaimed the Queen's Sovereignty over a tract of country between the Orange and Vaal Rivers, which was described by an early traveller as 'a howling desert,' but which has long since become the home of many prosperous farmers. The announcement that the hated authority was again placed over men who had migrated to be free from it, was received with the greatest indignation. Commandant-General Pretorius took command of the Boers, a little garrison at Bloemfontein was forced to capitulate, and when Sir Harry Smith, commanding in person, pushed on all the available forces of the colony over the Orange River to put down 'the rebellion,' he soon encountered the small army of the farmers at Boomplaats, and after a rather hot engagement forced them to retire. This battle was described by the English general as one of the 'most severe *skirmishes*' in which he had ever been engaged. Of course no further resistance was possible, and Her Majesty's Sovereignty was at once reproclaimed, and various officials appointed. On the 25th of March 1851, letters-patent were issued, creating a constitution which provided for a nominee Legislative Council. Major Warden, who had been appointed, called out a commando to clear the Caledon River district of Bushmen marauders, and the Batlokua natives had afterwards to be suppressed. The greatest difficulties, however, were encountered from the Basutos, whose chief was one of the most remarkable men who have helped to make history in South Africa. Moshesh was a diplomatic genius, full of astuteness and discernment of character. Personally, he desired to maintain peace, but his people, eager for plunder, frequently made war inevitable. They had harboured cattle stolen from our native allies, and when called upon to restore them, sent a herd of inferior description. A meeting of all chiefs was subsequently called at Bloemfontein, but Moshesh lamented his inability to attend, because of the confused and alarming state of affairs around him. A hurriedly collected and motley commando was sent out against the Basutos, and at what has been styled the battle of Viervoet this force was completely routed by the enemy under the command of Letsie, Molapo and Moperi. The Resident of the Sovereignty (Major Warden) had made a great mistake by meddling with inter-tribal contests among the natives. The Dutch farmers held aloof, and he was forced to obtain reinforcements from Natal and remain on the defensive. A republican party among the emigrants took advantage of what they considered an opportunity, and declared a republic at Winburg, while Moshesh, who in after years was remarkable for his professions of devotion to the Queen, declared that he would assist them.

Certainly the British position in South Africa at this time was uncomfortable. Sir Harry Smith, in the Cape Colony, was engaged in repressing Hottentots, Tembus and Xosas, while for the protection of countries then considered worthless, north of the Orange River, a considerable force involving great expenditure seemed necessary. Compromise appeared desirable, so when the emigrant farmers desired to come to a friendly understanding, they were listened to, and their independence, in a republic beyond the Vaal River, was acknowledged by an arrangement made on the 17th January 1852, which has ever since been known as the Sand River Convention. By this treaty, Commissioners guaranteed in the fullest manner on the part of the British

Government to the emigrant farmers beyond the Vaal River the right to manage their own affairs and to govern themselves according to their own laws.[1] Thus did they find at last a place of refuge, and what they believed would form a permanent home in the wide extended territories now dignified with the title of the South African Republic.

The country between the Orange and Vaal Rivers was, as has already been stated, supposed to be a dangerous encumbrance rather than a valuable acquisition. Moshesh and his Basutos had to be reckoned with as well as the Dutch Boers, and Sir George Cathcart's experience at the battle of Berea was by no means an agreeable one. He really had to retreat, and was most gratified when the wily chief of the Basutos astutely sued for peace. This was granted, and all the white people of the Sovereignty left to their own resources. There was an outcry and an appeal to the imperial authorities, but Her Majesty's Government, having to look on the surface and consider the impatience of British taxpayers, decided to withdraw from the Orange River Sovereignty. The cunning Moshesh took care to inform all the tribes with which he was in

[1] The full text is given in Theal's *History of the Boers*, p. 302.

communication that he had gained a great battle, and driven the English from his country, and thus laid the foundation of an extended reputation which greatly increased his power. Sir George Clerk was sent out in 1853 as a Commissioner to withdraw British authority from the Sovereignty with the best grace and in the best manner possible; and the extraordinary spectacle was witnessed of a high official, in order to carry out instructions, being compelled to make overtures to men who were recently accounted rebels. Frightful pictures of the calamities which the natives would have to endure if Boers ruled over the Sovereignty were painted by anti-slavery and missionary societies in England, and in the Cape Colony, abandonment was also strongly opposed. Nevertheless, the work had to be done. The territory was very distant, and thought to be utterly useless as well as extremely expensive. On investigation, many of the charges against the Boers could not be substantiated, but even if they did carry on qualified slavery, and look upon native tribes as the Israelites did upon the Hittites and Jebusites, it was too much to expect the British taxpayer to expend enormous sums in further contests with Basutos and emigrant farmers. A well-disposed assembly met at Bloemfontein, on the 23d of February 1854, when a convention was signed which transferred the government to representatives elected by the inhabitants; and the Orange Free State was founded.

# CHAPTER VIII

Sir George Grey—The Kafirs checkmated—Sir Philip Wodehouse—Discovery of Diamonds—The South African Republic—President Burgers—Sir Bartle Frere—Kafir War—Difficulties with Cetywayo—The Zulu War—Isandhlwana—Rorke's Drift—Ulundi—Blunders—Annexation of the Transvaal—War with the Boers—Sir George Colley and Majuba Hill—The Land of Goshen—Expansion.

A GREAT statesman grasped the helm of the State when Sir George Grey was appointed Governor and High Commissioner in 1854. He found the Cape Colony at the commencement of a new political career, with representatives of the people in two Houses of Parliament, a sparsely-peopled country in which sheep-farming was the principal pursuit, and a frontier constantly threatened by masses of turbulent and warlike natives. The cruel tortures inflicted by means of witchcraft were still undergone, and the domination of chiefs rendered the progress of civilisation hopeless. The new Governor quickly grasped the fact that avarice was as much a vice of savages as of Christians, and, by paying salaries to the chiefs, induced them to abandon their authority, which was put into the hands of magistrates. A strong police force and a system of espionage were established. By means of the latter every detail of the plot to kill all the cattle and then drive the hated white man into the sea was fully discovered. The necessary precautions were taken, and the result was that rebellion was made impossible, and 30,000 Kafirs died of starvation. The frontier districts were partially depopulated, and this gave a better opportunity for the location of the Anglo-German legion and a body of agricultural labourers from Germany. Sir George Grey was as enterprising in matters concerning the development of the colony as he was politic in concerting measures for its defence. Railways and a breakwater for Table Bay were commenced, and every possible effort was made to lay the foundation of an empire, whose expansion Sir George Grey foresaw.

Sir Philip Wodehouse became Governor in 1862, and was as conservative as his predecessor was progressive. British Kaffraria was incorporated with the Cape Colony in 1865, much against the wishes of its inhabitants.

and reactionary proposals for giving the executive increased power, and reducing the number of the representatives of the people, having been defeated, Sir Henry Burhly, who had considerable experience in the working of constitutional government in Australia, was appointed Governor in succession to Sir Philip Wodehouse. At this period the prospects of the expansion of Southern Africa were so unsatisfactory that one of the most eminent men who have ever held office in the country, the Hon. William Porter, was of opinion that no career of prosperity was before it. There had been war on the border, war between the Basutos and the Orange Free State, severe droughts causing enormous loss of sheep and cattle, the wine trade suffered under heavy depression, commercial matters were in a most unsatisfactory position, and, generally, the aspect of affairs was black enough to daunt the heart of the most enthusiastic patriot, It is always darkest in the hour before day. The dawn of prosperity arose when diamonds were discoverd near the Vaal River in 1869, and the full sunshine of success fell upon the country when, in 1871 and the years immediately following, the new dry diggings were opened at Kimberley, which soon yielded gems to the value of millions of pounds sterling per annum. Then business flourished, farmers obtained a market, and railways were extended beyond the Orange River to the new northern El Dorado.

The South African Republic, ruled as a democracy, with a House of the People's Representatives styled the 'Volksraad,' had been from the first distinguished by dissensions among its people, which sometimes culminated in civil war. The Boers love freedom from taxation in a super-eminent manner, and the Treasury was in a constant state of depletion, not improved by the premature and ambitious schemes of President Burgers. Golden coins were issued bearing his effigy, and railway material was imported only to lie unused on the shores of Delagoa Bay. None know better than the natives when opportunities exist, and the British authorities saw with grave apprehension an impoverished and badly governed state seriously threatened by the greatest savage power in South Africa. White inhabitants called out for speedy protection, and Lord Carnarvon, then Secretary of State for the Colonies, thought it wise to send Sir Theophilus Shepstone from Natal as a Special Commissioner, empowered with the approval of the High Commissioner, to annex any territory he might think fit to the British dominions. All this was foolish, as it did not take into account the unconquerable hatred of the bulk of the people of the Transvaal to English rule. It is true that Cetywayo threatened, but if we had waited a little longer the Boers would have asked us to help them, and this would have put an essentially different aspect on the position. As it was, we merely entered their country, took for granted what should never have been taken for granted—that is, the wishes of the mass of the people—and pensioning off the chief officials, declared that there was an end of that system of government for which the Voortrekkers had fought, and which was almost as dear as life to their descendants.

A tried and experienced Indian Administrator now appears upon the scene in the person of Sir Bartle Frere, who was appointed Governor of the Cape Colony, and Her Majesty's High Commissioner in the year 1877. The difficulties of his administration were numerous and serious. A Kafir war had to be encountered in the first instance when the Gcaleka chief, Kreli, in attacking the Fingoes and carrying off their cattle, came into collision with the colonial mounted police. The natives were speedily dispersed, and Sandilli, chief of the Gaikas, their ally, was slain. Then war in the field caused a fight in the Cabinet. Sir Bartle Frere showed that under a velvet glove his was an iron hand, and put an end to any opposition to his views by dismissing the Cabinet under Sir J. C. Molteno, the first Prime Minister of the Cape Colony, and entrusting the direction of affairs to Sir J. Gordon Sprigg.

The great storm which had long threatened the entire eastern portion of South Africa now burst, and the last, greatest, and most decisive struggle commenced between the natives and the Europeans. The conquests of the ferocious Chaka had driven no fewer than 100,000 fugitives to the westward of the Tugela River, and how to rule this vast and fast-increasing number became a difficult problem. In Natal the policy of the Government has always been to keep the coloured races distinct from the white population, and to govern them by their own laws through their own chiefs under one great chief, who was, of course, a British official. It was felt, that if a victorious army of Zulus crossed the Tugela, all the natives between that river and the Keiskamma would unite with them, and that the entire destruction of the white population of Natal would be almost inevitable. Cetywayo had resolved upon war, and cared little to conceal his determination. When a remonstrance was sent against the king's barbarous murder of young women, replies of extreme insolence were despatched to the Natal Government, at the same time solemn promises were distinctly denied, and the great monarch declared his intention of shedding blood on a grander scale than had been as yet attempted. One of his chiefs, named Sirayo, had the audacity to enter British territory, and to carry off two women who were British subjects, and when redress was demanded it was peremptorily refused. On the 13th of January 1879, the High Commissioner declared that the best had been done to avoid war by every means consistent with honour, and that he felt bound to use his power to secure future peace and safety. Lieutenant-General Lord Chelmsford, commanding the troops in South Africa, was then ordered to carry out this resolution.

Early in January 1879 the British troops, divided into four columns, crossed the Tugela, and invaded Zululand. Our army had entered a country in which the mountain sides are furrowed by deep kloofs or ravines. 'The Bush' in many places forms a natural fortress, in which the warlike native, panther-like, loves to lie in wait for his foe. The tactics of the Zulus were, however, on this occasion of a bold order. Their plan was, like Chaka, to fight and conquer by attacking in the form of a beast with horns, chest and loins. They usually make a feint with one horn, while the other, concealed by long grass or bush, sweeps round for the purpose of encompassing its enemy. The chest then advances, and endeavours by its vast power to crush opposition. The loins are kept at a distance, and only join in pursuit.

Unfortunately here, as elsewhere, we began by under-estimating the power of the enemy. The plan of 'laagering,' or so joining waggons together as to make an impregnable fort, seemed to have never been considered; or, if considered, dismissed as unworthy of attention. Yet this simple plan had rendered small bands of Voortrekkers invincible, and might have saved a regiment on the fatal day of Isandhlwana. We gained a battle at Inyezani, and then the portion of our troops which had been engaged continued their progress. On the 20th January 1879 the camp of the third column, comprising the 24th Regiment, with artillery, police, native contingent and volunteers, was encamped at the Isandhlwana mountain. Lord Chelmsford moved off to attack a force said to be fourteen miles distant; and in the meantime, on the fatal 22d January 1879, the Zulu army, 20,000 strong, consisting of the flower of Cetywayo's troops, moved in the first instance in small detached bodies to a position about a mile and a half to the east of the British camp. We were completely out-generalled. The foolish division of the British forces was known and appreciated; an opportunity was afforded and at once taken. In their usual strong formation, the entire Zulu army pounced down upon the unfortified camp. An attempt to check their progress was as feeble and unavailing as if it had been the advancing ocean tide which was combated. In spite of shells, of cannon balls, and of musketry, the steady advance of the Zulus continued. Three times was the Nkobamakosi Regiment repulsed, but the Inbonambi Regiment, coming up as a reinforcement, enabled the Zulus to rush forward along the south front of the camp and accomplish a turning movement. The camp was surrounded; overwhelming numbers crushed everything before them. In fact, as the sea irresistibly breaks on the land, so did the Zulu host invincibly advance with overwhelming power and strength. One of our great tragedies then occurred, when naked savages, advancing with frightful yells, relentlessly stabbed their victims with assegais. No mercy was asked nor given. Four hundred and five men of one battalion fell on the field of battle, and the name of the 24th Regiment is indissolubly linked with the greatest disaster the Imperial arms ever encountered in Southern Africa. The eclipse of the sun on that day was typical of the eclipse which British power, supremacy, and prestige suffered. The great plan of Sir Bartle Frere for the British flag to wave over a South African empire, extending from Capetown to the Zambesi, was shattered to atoms. The Transvaal Boers took heart of grace, and we may trace the loss of the country which contains the richest gold mines in the world to the events which naturally grew up from the terrible disaster of Isandhlwana. The immediate effects might have been too terrible almost to think of. A great conquering Zulu army entering Natal would have had reinforcements of 50,000 men shortly after they crossed the Tugela, and, like the devastating hordes of Attila, might have continued to gain new strength by conquest until, like a relentless torrent, it was able to pour its terrible force upon the Cape colony. Providentially there was an obstacle which, although it seemed feeble, proved thoroughly effective. At Rorke's Drift, on the Tugela River, Lieutenant Chard of the Royal Engineers commanded a small force, which included in its number a company of the 24th Regiment under Lieutenant Bromhead.

On the afternoon of the fatal 22d of January two men came furiously riding from Zululand to Rorke's Drift, and called aloud to be taken across the Tugela River. They lost no time in communicating to the officer in command at the little fort the news of the fatal disaster, which meant that a great Zulu army was rapidly advancing to the attack. Every effort was, of course, immediately made for defence. Bags of provisions had to be used as breastworks, waggons were interlaced, loopholes formed, and the brave little garrison determined to repulse the enemy or die behind their frail entrenchments. Within one hour and a quarter of the alarm being given, the vanguard force of the Zulus, 600 strong, advanced at a run against the south wall. Although they sustained very heavy fire, some of their number had to be driven off by the bayonet. A number of desperate assaults were resisted in the same way, and, unfortunately, the enemy was able to pour in a harassing fire from neighbouring rocks, which forced the garrison to retreat behind an entrenchment of biscuit boxes. The hospital was attacked and set in flames, desperate but ineffectual attempts were made to fire the stores, and shortly before darkness set in the gallant little force, which was fighting for their country and their own lives, was compelled to retire to the centre of the entrenchments. Until midnight they had to fight desperately, then the enemy relaxed their efforts and South Africa was saved.

The tide having been turned, flowed in favour of the British forces. The battle of Kambulu was gained, Lord Chelmsford marched into the heart of Zululand with 4000 men, and was able to defeat Cetywayo in a battle at Ulundi before his successor Lord Wolseley could arrive. Soon afterwards the great Zulu monarch was captured, all the influential chiefs gave in their submission, and, if wisdom had guided operations, Zululand would have been annexed to the empire. But the new disposer of events, as he could not take over the country by order of Downing Street, thought it wise to divide it into thirteen separate districts, each ruled by a kinglet. As might have been expected, this plan resulted in disorganisation, dissatisfaction and danger. Cetywayo was taken to England and became the African Lion of the hour, and then, as a culmination of foolishness, he was sent back to his country in order apparently that a sanguinary carnival should take place. However, after this had lasted some time, the king surrendered to the British power, and finally solved the cruel problem of what to do with him by his sudden death. The British Government only retained a 'Reserve,' so the neighbouring Boer farmers stepped in and formed 'a new Republic,' which eventually became incorporated with the Transvaal, while our portion has been added to Natal.

The Zulu war required British troops to be poured into South Africa at a great cost, but the war was really absolutely necessary for the expansion of South Africa, and its difficulties are principally to be attributed to the initial disaster at Isandhlwana. Sir Bartle Frere thoroughly understood the position, and although unfortunate and treated with that injustice which misfortune commonly receives, was both a true patriot and a wise statesman. He argued justly that it would have been vain, indeed almost criminal, to ignore the fact that there had grown up, by our sufferance, alongside Natal a very powerful military organisation, directed by an irresponsible, blood-thirsty and treacherous despot.[1] This extraordinary power simply made the existence of a peaceful English community so precarious as to prevent its safe continuance in any other form than that of an armed camp.

Men whose religion is to fight, and whose virtues bear proportion to the number of persons they kill, must necessarily be subdued or civilisation cannot go forward. The Voortrekkers found this to be the case with the sanguinary and treacherous Dingaan. Cetywayo and his armies belonged to the same class, while with the Zulus of Matabeleland it was also found, later on, that the teaching of Christianity was impossible, and that white men could not occupy the country unless the power of the savage was broken and his military organisation shattered. All South African his-

---

[1] Miss Colenso champions the Zulu people, and, no doubt, injustices have been done to them, nevertheless a war sooner or later could certainly not have been avoided, and the complete downfall of the reign of despots in Zululand and Matabeleland was a necessity for the progress of civilisation. See works by Miss Colenso for the views of her own and her father (Bishop Colenso) in favour of the Zulus.

tory teaches the lesson that, so far as aboriginal natives are concerned, you must either conquer or be conquered. There can be no compromise, and it is idle to talk as if wars were forced upon natives—they came as an absolute necessity, and without them the expansion of South Africa would have been impossible.

An unfortunate man is always in the wrong when responsible ministers are masters, and therefore Sir Bartle Frere was recalled, not listened to when his advice should have been asked, and, having served the nation as a patriot, received the usual reward of being neglected when living and honoured by a monument after his death.

> As if honour's breath could revive the silent dust,
> Or memory soothe the dull, cold ear of death.

The attention of the civilised world was drawn to Zululand when the terrible intelligence reached Europe of the death of the Prince Imperial. The heir of that brilliant dynasty, whose founder had conquered and awed nations, was stabbed to death by savages in a remote corner of distant Southern Africa. The Prince, being fond of hard work, and exceedingly daring, could scarcely be prevented from going out with patrols and on reconnaissance duty. At the commencement of June

1879 he was attached to the Quartermaster-General's department at General Newdigate's camp, and obtained leave to go in advance of his division. The reconnoitring party consisted of Lieutenant Carey, 98th Regiment, six men of Bettington's Horse, and one Kafir, all under the command of the Prince Imperial. A halting-place in a donga was chosen, where they off-saddled for an hour. During that time fifty Zulus crawled through the long grass, ready to make a spring, but one was seen by the Kafir attached to the British patrol, and he reported the circumstance to the Prince, who, unfortunately, only coolly remarked that he would give another ten minutes. All the horses were ready and saddled. Then came the words 'Prepare to mount,' 'Mount,' followed by a crashing volley fired from forty rifles at a distance of twenty yards. Immediately afterwards, with a tremendous cry of 'Usutu' and 'Lo, the English cowards!' the savages rushed on. The horses swerved, and some even broke away, while everyone who could spring on his horse did so and galloped off. There was one exception. The Prince Imperial's horse, which was sixteen hands high and always difficult to mount, became so frightened by the firing and stampede as to rear and prance in such a manner as to make it impossible for his master to mount. All rushed past, taking 'sauve qui peut' as their motto, and although the Prince strained every nerve to gain the saddle, his holster unfortunately gave way, and the excited horse, having trampled upon him, broke loose and ran away. Fourteen Zulus now advanced, and with the intrepidity of his race and country, the heir of the Napoleons died, never calling for help, and bravely, with his face to the foes, fighting courageously to the last. His first wound was mortal, and although the death of this noble and beloved scion of a great house was extremely lamentable, yet, nevertheless, there was some consolation in knowing that he did nothing in his last moments—as during his short career—either to sully the name he bore or the country which gave him birth. With all the marks of respect which were possible, the body of the deceased Prince was conveyed to D'Urban, Natal, and thence in H.M.S. *Boadicea* to England.[1]

The Basutos always gave trouble, and under Moshesh had been so successful, that they

---

[1] A full account of the circumstances attendant on the death and funeral of the Prince Imperial are contained in *The History of the Zulu War*, by A. Wilmot. London, 1880.

were emboldened to defy the Cape Colony in the year 1880, when they were unwisely called upon to deliver up their arms under the provisions of a Peace Preservation Act passed in 1877. More than a million pounds sterling were squandered, the war was a failure, and Basutoland had to be abandoned and placed under the control of the Imperial Government, since which time it has been benefited by a law excluding the sale of intoxicants. The people are now among the most sober and industrious in South Africa. The brandy interest in the western districts of the Cape find its principal market, almost its only market, among the native tribes of South Africa, and, as a consequence, new, badly-distilled, ardent spirits are spread broadcast among these people, to their serious detriment and that of the labour market of the country.

Unquestionably a blunder was committed by the annexation of the Transvaal to Great Britain, ratified by Lord Carnarvon on behalf of the Crown in 1887. As in the case of Isandhlwana, so in that of the South African Republic, the ignorance of our representatives was simply phenomenal. The mass of the people of Dutch extraction was indignant that the country which the Voortrekkers had shed their blood to acquire — the land of promise which the new Israelites had entered into—should be abandoned to the Pharaoh from whose bondage they had escaped. Lord Chelmsford seemed to have no information about Zulu movements previous to his great defeat, and our Shepstones and Carnarvons were content calmly to place a new and hated government upon the top of a volcano, under which the passions of hatred and the ardent desire of freedom furiously burnt. Deputations had gone to England, one of which bore memorials from 6000 inhabitants. No redress nor promise of redress could be obtained. The representative assembly promised them was not even granted, and when Sir Garnet Wolseley successfully stormed the stronghold of the chief Secocoeni, the Boers sullenly held aloof. The indiscreet actions of Sir Owen Lanyon, the Administrator of the Transvaal, at last filled the cup of the people's indignation to overflowing, and the members of the old Volksraad, which had not assembled since 1877, were summoned to meet at Paardekraal, now known as Krugersdorp, on 13th December 1880. Messrs Kruger, Joubert and Pretorius were appointed a triumvirate to carry on the government, large forces of burghers were levied, Pretoria as well as other towns garrisoned by English troops were invested, and a detachment of the 94th Regiment was attacked on the march, when no fewer than fifty-five men, as well as the commanding officer, were killed.

Sir George Colley, Governor of Natal and High Commissioner, saw an opportunity of which he determined to take the utmost advantage, but his zeal and headstrong courage unfortunately far exceeded either his experience or ability. He marched to the border with little more than one thousand men and six guns, but General Joubert, anticipating this movement, crossed at once into Natal and occupied the strong position of Lange's Nek. On the 28th of January 1881 the British troops attempted to storm this pass, but were met with a deadly fire from the well-directed guns of protected men, and were repulsed with heavy loss. At Ingogo Heights there was another disaster on the 7th of February. General Sir Evelyn Wood shortly afterwards arrived with reinforcements, and if he had been given time to come up, it is probable that the campaign would have assumed a different aspect; but while these troops were being hurried on, Sir George Colley, eager to retrieve his losses, with recklessness utterly unrelieved by any skill,

## Expansion of Southern Africa 165

marched out of camp at night with 400 men and occupied Majuba Hill, which overlooked the Boer camp. The 27th of February 1881 was another fatal day for the British arms in Southern Africa. A portion of the Dutch farmers' force ascended the hill and, taking advantage of capital cover afforded by rocks, drove the troops off. Sir George Colley, six officers and ninety men were killed, and Commandant General Joubert was able to report that 'the troops fought like true heroes, but God gave us the victory.' The knell of British supremacy was now sounded; for although 10,000 troops were ordered out, and the greatest British general of the day appointed to command them, General Roberts was recalled, and a convention ratified at Pretoria on the 25th of October 1881, guaranteeing complete self-government to the people of the Transvaal, subject to the suzerainty of the Queen. The truth is that the British taxpayer was not prepared to spend millions on a new South African war, particularly when the country was not considered worth fighting for. It is true that Mr Gladstone said that if the territory were 'as valuable as it was worthless, the same policy would have been adopted;' and it must be admitted that, before the engagement at

Majuba Hill, President Brand of the Orange Free State, when exercising his influence in favour of peace, was supported by the Home Government ordering Sir George Colley to suspend hostilities if the Boers would cease fighting, in order that a scheme might be developed for granting them self-rule. Eventually, in 1884, the suzerain rights were relinquished, and all responsibility for the internal management of the affairs of the state entirely abandoned—the right alone being reserved of veto over any treaties with other countries, with the one exception of the Orange Free State. It also prescribed complete religious toleration, but the Roman Catholics and Jews, nevertheless, are debarred from holding office in a country which styles itself a Republic.

Native chiefs are the catspaws of governments as well as of concessionaires, and disputes between Batlapin, Barolong and Koranna chiefs served to illustrate this fact. Mankaraone and Montsioa came under British rule as their status was recognised by the Keate award, but Massouw and Moshette were ranged on the other side favoured by the protection of the Transvaal Republic. Now, there was an opportunity for freebooters to take side and fight after the fashion of the freelances of the middle ages. The allies of Massouw formed a small but 'free and independent' Republic which they styled 'Stellaland'; and those of Moshette, not to be outdone, formed another state on the same plan, to which they gave the inviting name of 'Goshen.' The members of the Convention of London saw the absolute necessity of keeping open a great British trade route to the north, and as a means to this end, as well as for the purpose of stopping inter-tribal disputes, an extension of the Transvaal territory was provided for, so as to place Mashouw and Moshette within its limits, and at the same time a British Protectorate was established over Montsioa, Mankaroane and the rest of the Bechuana tribe. Nevertheless, the Goshen freelances sallied forth against the town of Mafeking, belonging to Montsioa; and shortly afterwards, as this chief had foolishly called in Commandant Joubert as a mediator, the South African Republic assumed jurisdiction over him and his people. The British Government immediately protested against this violation of the convention, and a force of 4000 men, including 2000 irregular cavalry, was sent up under Sir C Warren, R.E., who established peace and order throughout Bechuanaland, and effectually put an end to any claims in that direction on the part of the South African Republic, which had promptly withdrawn its annexation proclamation when it was seen that a war with Great Britain might be the result. A further expansion of British territory took place in the year 1885, when the British Protectorate was declared to extend over Bechuanaland and the Kalihari. A Crown colony, styled British Bechuanaland, was formed in the country south of the Molopo River.

## CHAPTER IX

Natal again—Representative Institutions, Populations, etc.
—The Orange Free State—Brief Sketch of History—
Griqualand West as a separate Crown Colony—Incorporation with the Cape Colony — Cape Events —
Germany in Damaraland—The Matabele Nation—
Chaka and Lo Bengula.

NATAL was divided into six counties in the year 1850, and in the two chief towns, D'Urban and Pietermaritzburg, municipal institutions were established. In 1856 a new constitution, including a legislative council, whose members were elected by the people, was conferred upon this colony, whose total white population had then reached 8500. Considerable enterprise was shown in pushing forward sugar and other industries, but tea planting seems now to be more successful than any other undertaking. Disturbances with the Amahlubi tribe under the chief Langalibalele were successfully repressed, and although the local government sat, metaphorically, upon a gunpowder magazine, no spark of insurrection was seriously feared until the war with Cetywayo broke out. Natal has been described by no less an authority than Mr Cecil Rhodes as a forwarding agency in the midst of a Kafir location, because of its special dependence on the carrying trade to the new El Dorado which has arisen in the South African Republic. A railway is soon to connect it with Johannesburg, but even then it will not have only to fight the Midland line from Port Elizabeth, but the much shorter one, now nearly finished, from Delagoa Bay *via* Pretoria.

The responsible government of the little sister colony is of very recent formation, and under it there are two houses of parliament. The entire white population has increased to 42,000. The Indian coolies, imported for sugar cultivation, number 43,000, while the aboriginal tribes comprise 469,000 souls. There has been perhaps more bravery than discretion in a handful of white people taking upon them the terrible responsibilities of managing half a million of the descendants of Moselikatze and other warlike champions of the Zulu and Kafir races. It must be admitted, however, that the destruction of the power of Cetywayo, and, last of all, the great successes of the Chartered Company with Maxim guns, leaves little to be feared. Nevertheless, the black races in Southern Africa have been increasing, and are now multiplying in a quicker ratio than white people. So much so is this the case, that there is some reason for contending that coloured people may yet dominate this vast country now in course of being opened for enterprise. Our European brethren must help us. They have congested populations panting for employment, full of enterprise, in many cases battling even for food. In the vast regions whose history we are recording, there is ample room in all descriptions of healthful country for that human energy which is dashing itself in old countries against the bars of restriction.

The Orange Free State is separated by the Orange River from the Cape Colony, and by the Vaal River from the South African Republic. Early this century it was partially occupied by murderous bands of marauders, who were designated Bergenaars, and, while carrying on a war against the Bushmen, constantly plundered the stock of the Bechuanas, and killed those who resisted. The Boers were too strong for these 'noble savages,' and thus added to the list of wrongs which, it is stated, they inflicted on the native races. The central portion of the country was uninhabited, and there white settlements were made. In 1835-6 the large number of farmers who cast off the dust of a British colony from their feet organised a government, which they styled a company, and formed their headquarters at Winburg. They soon came into contact with the half-caste Griquas, the latter of whom were assisted by the British Government, when Sir Perigrine Maitland intervened in 1845 and dispersed the Boers at Zwartkoppies. A British Resident was appointed, and the whole territory was subsequently annexed to the Empire under the title of the Orange Free State Sovereignty. Already we have adverted to the unsuccessful attempt of the unfortunate farmers to retain their own form of government. Their defeat at Boomplaats in 1848 by Sir Harry Smith caused them to retreat further into the interior. These haters of arbitrary power trekked to that country beyond the Vaal, which was yet to become wealthy and world-renowned under the name of the South African Republic. 'Like arrows in the hand of the mighty so are the children of those cast out' has been fully and bitterly exemplified in the case of the emigrant Boers of the Cape Colony, who have handed down from father to son traditional hatred of that empire which,

## Expansion of Southern Africa 173

in their opinion, drove them forth by injustice to seek homes in the desert.

The Orange River Territory, being looked upon as troublesome, worthless, and likely to lead the British taxpayer into difficulties, was abandoned in 1854, and has since been the Orange Free State, well and wisely governed as a Republic, under a President and Volksraad at Bloemfontein. Strange irony of fate; the cast-off States have given their former masters great reasons to regret abandoning them. The Transvaal becomes one of the greatest gold-mining countries in the world; and the Orange Free State showed itself about 1869 to contain mines of diamonds more rich, vast and wonderful than any described in Oriental tales. There is no doubt that the great dry diggings at Kimberley were all really within the Free State boundary. The Republic in due course sent its officers to exercise jurisdiction; but then conveniently arose the claim of the Griqua chief, Waterboer, ceded to the British Government, and accepted by it. Griqualand West was formed, and the Boers saw themselves again robbed of their territory, simply because it was worth taking. The weaker Government had, of course, to submit; but eventually Her Majesty's Secretary of

State, Lord Carnarvon, paid £90,000 as a most inadequate 'compensation,' and offered a further sum of £15,000 to encourage the construction of railways.

The fevered life of 'Griqualand West' as a separate Crown colony was of brief duration. The first diamond was picked out of river pebbles collected by a farmer's child from the bed of the Orange River, in the Hope Town division of the Cape Colony. In 1870 the first dry digging was discovered, and a Port Elizabeth firm purchased the famous Vooruitzight Estate for £6000, and re-sold it to the Colonial Government for £100,000. Numbers of claims were marked out, sold and re-sold; a big mining camp sprung up, which grew into the town of Kimberley, and a Lieutenant-Governor, with a Secretary and Council, endeavoured to evoke order out of the chaos of a motley mining population. Disturbances occurred, and troops were sent up to quell them. Then came trying times, when diamonds fell and shares were at a discount. A master spirit then rose in South Africa, whose first successes were in discerning the cause of these disasters and applying a remedy. He saw that unless the diamond market were controlled there could be no hope of success. Diamonds to the amount of several millions annually were obtained from very numerous mines, and the only way to prevent utter collapse was consolidation. This man was Mr Cecil Rhodes, an English gentleman, who came, after a University education, to seek health in South Africa, and, after farming experiences not remarkable for success, found himself among the fortune-seekers at the new El Dorado. He allied himself to the De Beers Mining Company, founded in 1880 with a capital of £200,000, which by degrees absorbed most of its smaller neighbours, till by the end of March 1885 its capital was raised to £841,000. Going on with its policy of amalgamation, steadily directed by Mr Rhodes, its capital in 1888 exceeded £2,250,000. At last lengthy negotiations resulted in the diamond-producing mines of De Beers, Kimberley, Du Toits Pan and Bultfontein being practically under the control of the great De Beers Consolidated Company, at a cost of £14,500,000, a great part of which was paid by means of debentures. The revenue of this company now exceeds £3,000,000 per annum, and it is estimated that £100,000 per month is spent by the company in Kimberley. The scale of operations is very large, and the machinery used of the best possible description. By means of regulating the market, prices are kept up to a mark which enables the mines to be worked. It is true that at one time 12,000 men were at work, when now perhaps only a third of the number is employed; but it is better to go on steadily with a comparatively small output than to carry on operations extensively and collapse. Griqualand West was in due course incorporated with the Cape Colony, of which it is now as much an integral part as the division of Stellenbosch.

The Orange River Free State, ruled wisely and well, has ever given true freedom to its inhabitants, and, under an enlightened system of government, has now obtained without cost or risk a yearly income of £160,000 per annum from railways made by the Cape through its territories. It had, however, its days of difficulties and of dangers, when the wily Moshesh fought with his Basutos against its burghers, and, becoming utterly defeated, threw himself upon British clemency, and obtained the proclamation of British sovereignty and protection over the country since known as Basutoland. The progress of this little Free State has been satisfactory. Up to 1870 its annual revenue did not exceed £70,000, but in 1886 it had risen to about £200,000 per annum. It has now a share in customs dues collected at colonial ports as well as of railway profits. It occupies an extensive table-land about 400 miles in length, having a breadth of 200 miles, with an altitude above sea level of between 4000 and 5000 feet, and its great undulating plains extend

> In airy undulations,
> As if the ocean in its gentlest swell
> Stood still, with all his rounded billows fixed
> And motionless for ever.

The white population is greater than that of Natal, as it comprises 77,000 people of European descent, and the natives only number 13,000. An excellent Parliament (Raad) guides and governs both the State President and the State. Here, indeed, there is a Republic where 'religion is free and conduct only amenable to law.'

To write the detailed history of the Cape Colony during the latter portion of the nineteenth century would require lengthy references to politics of but small interest in Europe. Representative and responsible institutions have worked fairly well, and though very much has yet to be done, the statute book is filled with good laws, and the development of the country by railways has been successfully

attempted. About 2000 miles of iron roads have cost £20,000,000, but the interest is fully paid by the railway revenue, and a balance remains to the credit of the taxpayer. In 1893 all the lines taken together paid £4, 16s. 8d. per cent., and at the present time 3½ per cent. Cape of Good Hope debentures are quoted in London at 107. These are extremely significant facts, which show what the mining centres have already done for South Africa; for, indubitably, without the diamonds of Kimberley and the gold mines of Johannesberg, no line of railway would even yet exist as far north as the Orange River. The internal development of the country is, however, very backward. No country requires irrigation more on an extensive scale, and in none would well-developed irrigation schemes pay better, but this source of wealth has been comparatively neglected. The whole strain has been in one direction—that of obtaining the transport of the goods and passengers of other states. This has been also the fault of Natal.

In July 1890 the ministry of Sir J. Gordon Sprigg was defeated on a question of launching heavy schemes of railway construction, and Mr Cecil J. Rhodes, member of the Legislative Assembly for Barkly, grasped the helm of the state, and, with a change in *personnel*, remains at the present moment Prime Minister of the Cape Colony.

'*E pluribus unum*' seems to be his motto. We have already seen him uniting interests at the diamond fields so as to form one great consolidated company, able to control the market, and therefore strong enough to keep mines constantly at work which would certainly otherwise have collapsed. We must now regard him as an empire-maker, stretching forth imperial sway from the land of Lo Bengula to the borders of the great African lakes.

Sir Henry Loch succeeded Sir Hercules Robinson as Governor of the Cape Colony and Her Majesty's High Commissioner. Both men have been indefatigable in doing their duty. The latter still holds the reins of Government, and with great judgment and tact steers the bark of British authority amidst rocks of republics, jealous colonies, native questions, and joint-stock company claims.

South Africa has been the Rip Van Winkle of the world, as, although colonised in 1652, it seemed to be asleep for more than 200 years, and only wakened up to a new life and new conditions towards the close of the nineteenth century. The greatest expansion of British rule in Africa that has yet taken place occurred within the last eight years. Many events led up to it, and it must be admitted that the '*auri sacra fames*' has been the principal motive power. Herr Mauch proclaimed the existence of gold in Matabeleland many years ago, but his voice was of one crying in the wilderness; nevertheless, his discoveries induced Thomas Baines to turn his attention to the subject, to obtain a concession from Lo Bengula, and to send home specimens of quartz which, when assayed in London, proved to be exceedingly rich. Nothing, however, was done by the syndicate who obtained this concession. In the course of time, in 1885, the extension of sovereignty over British Bechuanaland and the country to the Zambesi was followed in 1888 by a treaty of peace concluded with Lo Bengula in his capacity as King of Matabeleland whereby, among other stipulations, it was agreed that this potentate should be debarred from entering into any treaty or correspondence with foreign powers without the sanction of Her Majesty's High Commissioner.

Very slight reference is necessary to the action of Germany in Damaraland. The Cape Colony retained the possession of Walvisch Bay, and, consequently, the great European power, ruled by our Queen's grandson, is very much hampered by the want of a seaport. Their operations have been hitherto conducted in a half-hearted manner, and certainly have not been very successful. The country itself is suitable for cattle raising, and is conjectured to be rich in mineral resources, but no emigration to it worthy of the name has yet taken place, and constant struggles with native chiefs have hitherto almost exclusively occupied the attention of the small force which garrisons this extensive country.

The rise and fall of the Matabele nation is one of the unknown chronicles of an almost unknown land,[1] but it is fraught with romance and interest. The valley of the Buffalo River in Zululand is the cradle of one of the most sanguinary races which ever desolated mankind. Umzilegazi was so called because of his father having been killed in battle, and because wherever he went blood (ogazie) fell in the track of his footsteps. Chaka, the great marauder, then ruled, and he contended that no man should be king unless he won the throne by his assegai.

[1] The important information embodied here is taken from a lecture by Mr Dennis Doyle, delivered in Grahamstown, but never published in Europe. This gentleman lived among the Matabele at Buluwayo, and knows the language and customs of the people intimately.

This man has been correctly styled as the Napoleon of South Africa, as his conquests extended to the Zambesi, and, in 1824, he appointed Umzilegazi commander of the home forces, while he went forth to slaughter in Natal and Pondoland. This lieutenant had only waited for an opportunity, and now, with 12,000 warriors and all the women and children of the nation, marched upwards through Swaziland into Matabeleland, where he quickly killed or enslaved the peaceful agricultural inhabitants. On Chaka's return to Zululand, he was violently enraged at the conduct of his Induna, and led his powerful army against him, but Umzilegazi, having been warned by the Swazies, trekked into the beautiful Marico division of the Transvaal, where to the present day his descendants are known as the Amandebele, or naked people with shields. Here their armies made desolate the neighbouring districts, although they departed from the usual custom of killing women and children, and substituted slavery for death. Umzilegazi's son by his first royal wife was named Kuruman, but another child was born in Marico in 1831, and was given the name of Lo Bengula, or one 'driven by the wind.'

The power of Chaka was feared by Umzilegazi, but that of the Voortrekkers made him flee beyond the Limpopo. At first, he established himself beside the Tati goldfields, but eventually chose a fertile, well-watered and healthy country not far distant, and then he declared that his son Lo Bengula should be his successor. Constant raids went on against the unfortunate Mashonas, who were hunted down like wild beasts; infamous savage customs and superstitions were carried on, and a writer who has lived in the country and well understands the language and manners of the people states that, although missionaries were established for more than thirty years among the Zulus, he is not aware that they made a single convert beyond those natives who were servants to clergymen. Umzilegazi listened on one occasion to a religious discourse concerning a future state, and asked at its conclusion, pointing to the subject Bakahla people, 'Then what will become of these slaves?' and when he was told that they also could be saved, cried out, 'Then I do not want to be a Christian.'

In 1868 'the mountain had fallen,' or, in other words, Umzilegazi was dead, and some time afterwards, when the death of Kuruman had been proved, Lo Bengula was proclaimed king, but the Zwangandaba retired from the council, and declared that they would never pay homage to the son of a Swazie woman. As the rebel faction was resolute, the new king proceeded to attack them, and when he bravely rode before their lines, was received with a storm of bullets. A desperate fight ensued, and Lo Bengula was the conqueror. Then, to commemorate this victory, the kraal of Buluwayo, or 'the one to be slain,' was formed. The first regiment of the kingdom was now ordered out to blood their spears, and a tribe in the north-west was designated as their victims, whom they then proceeded to murder with that sanguinary fury which is a type of exalted virtue among savages. But perhaps nothing can better indicate the absolute cruelty of the race better than the conduct of Lo Bengula to his own sister, with whom for years he had lived on terms of friendship and affection. Nina, as she was called by the Europeans, was his constant companion, ate out of the same dish, and exercised a powerful and favourable influence over him. Suddenly she was accused of witchcraft, taken away a few hundred yards, and strangled in the light of day by the order of her own brother. When led to execution, one of the most dramatic scenes recorded in South African history took place. This princess, who had long borne sway over the mind of the king, knew full well that jealousy had caused her destruction, so, on the way to execution, she turned to the queens, and in an awful manner, raising her hand to heaven, invoked a terrible curse upon them, and swore by Matshobana that no child of Lo Bengula, born of a Gaza woman, would ever sit on the throne of the Matabele. From that day not one of these women brought forth a child.

The death of his own sister seemed only to whet the king's appetite for blood. His brother, being like him, was once mistaken for him, consequently witchcraft was introduced and the culprit slain. Numbers of other relations were also killed, and to be akin to Lo Bengula was to be in the most dangerous position in the country. It is, of course, impossible to furnish a catalogue of the merciless acts of this monster, who has received the sympathy of thousands of philanthropic subjects of Her Majesty in England, but notice should be taken of the atrocious murder of Umhlaba, the Vice-Regent, and most of his family in 1892. The man whose father had saved the life of the king was sacrificed to a ferocious jealousy which regarded neither gratitude nor justice.[1]

The lost tribe of Umpezeni was sought for and found, mixed up with the Mashonas as one people. Relying on promises of protection, they cultivated their fields, and collected together a few cattle and goats. Down came the wolf on the fold, men were killed, women enslaved, and the country turned into a desolate waste. In 1888 Messrs Rudd, Maguire and Thomson obtained the celebrated gold con-

---

[1] The ideal set before the Zulu or Matabele was exactly the ideal set before the Greeks of Homer and the Norsemen of the Sagas—

> A heathen horde,
> Reddening the sun with smoke, and earth with blood,
> And on the spike that split the mother's heart,
> Spitting the child.
> (Tennyson's *Coming of Arthur*, p. 5, ed. 1869.)

To the Viking, the way of plunder, murder and massacre in this life led to happiness in the next with Odin in Valhölla. While Homer makes Odysseus boast of his dreadful work when he says (*Odyssey* I., 39-42), 'A breeze, bearing me away from Ilium, brought me to the Ciconeans to Ismarus: there I sacked their city, and destroyed the men, after taking their wives and much property out of the city.' Writing of such deeds, Thucydides (1.5) declares that 'such occupation, in no respect having disgrace attached to it, rather bringing somewhat of glory with it.' Of no nation in the world, ancient or modern, can the following words in Guinevere be more fitly applied than to the kings of the Zulu race:—

> The children born of thee are sword and fire,
> Red ruin and the breaking up of laws,
> The craft of kindred, and the godless hosts
> Of heathen swarming.

cessions which became the foundation of a royal charter to the British Africa Company. But it was at first thought that the great Queen disapproved. To make this right, the magnificent appearance and uniform of officers and men of the Horse Guards were spectacularly used, and Lo Bengula succumbed to the splendour of plumes, helmets and cuirasses. A queen's letter in such hands was sufficient. Then came the pioneer force, which successfully penetrated to Salisbury, led by the traveller Selous, under the military command of Colonel Pennefather. Why did not the king then strike? A writer, thoroughly conversant with the subject, partially replies to the question when he tells us that the stern rule of former days had been relaxed, and offences once punishable by death were now openly committed. Nevertheless, the young Matabele warriors clamoured to be led against the white man. They were accustomed to hunt the Mashonas like game, and foolishly believed that their forces were invincible. The writer already quoted (Mr Dennis Doyle) says, ' I have spent hours and days in endeavouring to convince the men of the Umbezo and other regiments that any conflict with us would mean certain defeat to the Matabele. They would listen with an amused smile, and remark, 'Well, before we pay tribute, we will fight, and then we will see who is best.' Extraordinary repetitions and analogies in history! Chaka was the first Napoleon of Southern Africa, Lo Bengula was the third. The latter felt that he must be ruined, delayed the fatal day as long as he could, but at last was borne away to destruction by the foolishness and enthusiasm of his own people.

The ferocious Zulu has been the invariable curse of this portion of the African continent. They depopulated Magaliesberg and Marico, two of the most fertile districts of a beautiful country. They entered no land which they did not fill with destruction, murder and rapine.[1] The Mashonas were so systematically hunted and killed that a well-peopled country became

---

[1] One of the most recent books on South-Eastern Africa, by Mr Selous, gives us the following significant facts which came under the personal observation of the author :—

'When the Matabele came, filing out in long lines across the open plain, in which Gazuma is situated, the Bushmen all ran away into the forest, with the exception of a few who took refuge in Africa's hut. One man and his wife, a woman with a young child at her breast, remained outside in the enclosure which surrounded the principal hut, saying that the Matabele would not interfere with Georos's, as Georos was Lo Bengula's friend. They helped themselves to meat, and then one of the Indunas asked some questions, and then plunged his assegai through the body of the baby and into the breast of the woman,

a desolate waste. The Zulus, in fact, were a perpetual barrier to peace and civilisation, but their turn had come when the British flag waved over the forts of the Chartered Company.

The question soon became perfectly clear. Was Lo Bengula and his braves to continue the scourge and ruin of the country or to be thoroughly conquered? The Matabele themselves knew that this was the real issue, as has already been indicated, and the young men of the army, who believed that the only reason for their existence was to shed blood, continued to raid and kill in the neighbourhood of the whites. Outrage followed outrage, and if impunity had been much longer permitted, the Europeans would then have been attacked and murdered.

killing them both with the one thrust. He then stabbed the man through the arm and the muscles of the chest, just as he turned to run, calling out at the same time, " Kill that dog." '

. . . . . . . . . .

Another instance may be given of the faithlessness and brutality of the Matabele :—

' At Khamas Wagon they also captured a Bushman, and told him his life should be spared if he would guide them to Pandamatenka. They struck the waggon road about fourteen miles from their destination, and then, knowing where they were, felt that they had no need of their guide, and assegaied him. "Three years afterwards, in 1888," says Mr Selous, " I was shown the spot where his remains had long lain at the foot of an ant heap, just at the side of the waggon track."'

# CHAPTER X

*The Key to Native Politics—Religion—Lo Bengula—The Great Northern Gold Fields—Zimbabye—Monomotapa and Ancient Gold Diggings—The Chartered Company's Pioneers' March—Mashonaland—Difficulties with the Portuguese.*

THE key to native politics and native proceedings in Southern Africa is a knowledge and appreciation of the religion of the natives and the machinery of witchcraft, by means of which it is practised. There is a very vague idea about a supreme being, but a very definite belief in the influence of the spirits of ancestors. The witch doctors are the mediums, and fulfil the threefold office of doctor, priest and soothsayer. They possess a knowledge of subtle and powerful poisons, so frequently used that everyone who gives food to another takes part himself to prove that it contains nothing hurtful. Necessarily, men who are believed to have full power over the invisible world, possess enormous influence, which is made use of by chiefs and powerful men for the purpose of destroying enemies and promoting schemes of war and plunder. A youth who aspires to be enrolled among the 'Isamesi' gives early signs of being destined for the office. He dreams of the spirits of the departed chiefs of his people, sees visions, falls into fits of frenzy, seeks out medicinal roots, and goes for instruction to experienced Isamesi. At last, what is called 'a change in the moon' takes place within him, he becomes a medium, fitted and enabled to hold converse with spirits.[1] The Zulu Government is despotic in an extreme degree, as the king's will is law and

[1] One of the greatest authorities, Mr Warner, says (*Kafir Races*, p. 287), 'It is impossible to suppose that these priests are not to a considerable extent self deceived, as well as the deceivers of others; and there is no difficulty to one who believes the Bible to be a divine revelation, in supposing that they are also to a certain extent under Satanic influence; for the idolatrous and heathen nations of the earth are declared in the inspired volume to be, in a peculiar manner, under the influence and power of the devil.' The Hon. Mr Godlonton in his *Case for the Colonists* gives us details of a case of torture, which is quoted merely as a specimen—'Although this poor victim implored for death, it was not granted to him until he had been literally roasted. Red-hot stones were placed on his groin, and when they slipped off, were held in position by means of sticks.' Another very common torture is that of smearing a victim, and then allowing him to be slowly eaten up by black ants or scorpions, whose thousand bites and stings produce lingering and excruciating torture. Roasting to death over a slow fire, so as to torture the unhappy victim for many hours, is very frequently resorted to.

he has unlimited power of life or death. Of course, his power is maintained by his soldiers, and to make them invulnerable the great national sacrifice of the 'Ukukufula' is made, when flesh is cut off the shoulder of a living beast and roasted on a fire into which certain charms have been thrown. Each man bites off a mouthful, while the unfortunate animal is left in torture.

Lo Bengula, although master of everyone in his country and a terror to neighbouring tribes, became unable to control the fierce military spirit which, like the vampire of story, continually required feasts of blood. Like another Frankenstein, he raised up a monster which he could not master, and which eventually destroyed him. Although so ruthless as to cause the death of his own sister, and utterly regardless of human life, as well as foully superstitious, he nevertheless saw the advantage of keeping on good terms with white men, from whom he was shrewd enough to obtain many gifts. He was sufficiently astute to pose before them as a man who kept his word and who was desirous of protecting them. It was, of course, his interest to do so, but we shall find that eventually his power was inadequate.

The newest gold country in the world was soon seen to be the oldest. Mauch, Barnes and other explorers found extensive ancient workings, and the vague reports which from time to time reached the outer world about pre-historic ruins were fully confirmed when we received full particulars concerning a subject of world-wide archæologic interest in the remains of the very ancient fort and temple of Zimbabye. Situated on a granite hill, with walls from sixteen to thirty-five feet high, and enclosing large and small stone towers, this conundrum from antiquity challenges solution. The work is rude and unsymmetrical, no written characters have been found engraved on the soapstone beams embedded in the walls or on the large flat stones standing upright on the floor. 'Lozenge-shaped and herring-bone patterns are carved, which agree exactly with the ornamentation on the outside,' and, as Mr Selous says,[1] 'More curious still, not alone with the patterns carved on the wooden knife sheaths, and scored on the pottery of the natives all over Mashonaland at the present day, but also with the patterns used in ornamenting the household utensils of all kinds in the

[1] Address before Royal Geographical Society.

Barotse Valley hundreds of miles away.' The circular building is a specimen of the ancient Phallic temple, where possibly Baal was worshipped when King Solomon ruled in Jerusalem. In the hill fortress there are pedestals of steatitic rock decorated with carved figures of carnivorous birds — ravens and hawks—sacred to the gods, of which they are symbols. Fragments of bowls were found here ornamented with figures of men and of animals, also native implements, bits of Persian glass, ingot moulds, and small crucibles. It has been proved by careful measurement that the builders of the temple adopted a geometric plan, and that it was oriented for observation of northern hemisphere stars. A series of curves with radii of various lengths formed the encircling wall; the cubit or length of the forearm was evidently the unit of measure, and the diameter of the great tower was exactly equal to the circumference of the small one. The radius or the diameter, or halves of them, and the curves of every wall can be found by multiplying the diameter of the building by the ratio of the circumference of a circle to its diameter, or by its square or cube.[1] The

[1] We know that the ruins of several large forts similar to those at Zimbabye, exist So recently as June 1894, Dr Sauer, Captain

people who worked for gold and worshipped Baal at Zimbabye were of Sabæan (South Arabian) or Phœnician origin. These two great maritime people of remote antiquity are the earliest maritime nations of whom there is a record. Sheba of Yemen was their emporium, and in the books of Jeremiah, Ezekiel and Isaias, as well as in Assyrian

<small>Sampson and Mr Bradley returned to Buluwayo from a long inspection in the south-east, in the course of which they discovered and explored a large ruined fortification, oval-shaped, with six layers of terraces, built of round granite, and distant only fifty miles from Buluwayo. The solid boulders are filled in with rubble, and there are the usual lines of ornamentation. The size of the structure is 200 feet in length, with a breadth of 300 feet and a height of 50 feet. Within a comparatively recent period it has been occupied by Arabs, whose huts, utensils and arms remain. Quoting further from the accounts furnished at the time, the finders tell us that near 'Fort Regina'—for so they have named the great ruin—they found a small Arab fort 100 yards away, evidently taken and burnt by natives. In round huts they found remains of charred pottery, smelted beads, silver, copper utensils, gold ornaments, with a large quantity of chains, beads and rings. Over fifteen ounces of splendid alluvial reef gold was discovered, as well as several nuggets weighing from one quarter to half an ounce, evidently traded from natives. 'The gold is of high quality from several different localities, but proving conclusively that there must be alluvial fields somewhere near, and richer quartz reefs than have yet been discovered.' We are further told that all old natives found there still remember when the Arabs were driven out by Umpezeni, a refugee Zulu chief who fled from the south up Sabi River with his women, men and cattle, and conquered the then great Mashona chief Marbo, under whose protection the Arabs were trading, Umpezeni afterwards being driven over the Zambesi by Moselikatze, where his people still remain.</small>

inscriptions at Nineveh, their widespread fame is chronicled. It was the Queen of the Sabæans who brought 120 talents of gold to Solomon, and it is probable that a portion, if not the whole, of this treasure was extracted from those old workings which now challenge curiosity and awake cupidity at the close of the nineteenth century of the Christian era.

The Arabs knew the secret carefully concealed by the Sabæans, and were continuing their traffic on the East African coast when the Portuguese arrived; but we naturally ask How did the country pass back into savagery from a state of comparative civilisation? Where are the remains of the ruined cities? There are none, and it is utterly a mistake to speak of 'ruined cities of Mashonaland.' As Mr Selous points out, there is no trace of any ancient town built of stone. The people lived near the great temples in huts plastered with mud, and the immense holes in the ground close at hand were dug to obtain clay for their pottery, and for the purpose of daubing their huts. Similar holes are invariably found at the side of any Bantu village at the present day. The blood of the ancient worshippers of Baal still runs in the veins of the people of the country. After a certain lapse of time the old heathenism gave way to the more modern spiritualism or worship of ancestors, the wall-building art was handed down and practised, gold mining was still carried on, but in a very modified manner, and then, as the Huns and northern barbarians came to the Roman empire, so came Umzilegazi, and the Zulus to the peaceful, industrious and unwarlike Mashonas. There really never was a highly-civilised people in South-Eastern Africa until the European races arrived. Gold mining went on without interruption until within one hundred years ago, and, putting fanciful theories aside, it seems fairly well established that a small number of ancient traders who were not highly civilised became by degrees merged in the mass of the inhabitants.[1]

Into the land of ancient mines and of rich quartz reefs entered stray hunters and explorers. Some of them knew, from various sources of information, that this was con-

[1] On this Zimbabye subject see Bent's *Ruined Cities of Mashonaland;* also works of Dr Slichter; F. C. Selous's 'Addresses to the Royal Geographical Society;' also *Travel and Adventure in South-East Africa,* by F. C. Selous; and *Matabeleland, the War, and our Position in South Africa,* by A. R. Colquhoun, first Administrator of Mashonaland.

jectured to be the Ophir of the ancients, and it certainly was the Monomotapa of the sixteenth century maps 'rich in gold.' A German explorer, named Mauch, found old workings and modern reefs. Thomas Baines became a friend of Lo Bengula, and obtained a concession of the right of working for gold throughout Matabeleland; but all speculations and syndicates were vain until, as a result of negotiations, on the 30th day of October 1888 'at my royal kraal,' the king gave 'the complete and exclusive charge over all metals and minerals to Charles Dunell Rudd of Kimberley, Rochfort Maguire of London, and Francis Robert Thompson of Kimberley, for a payment of £100 per month, 1000 breech-loading rifles with cartridges, and a gunboat for the Zambesi.' Subsequently this concession was united to another one connected with land ownership. Various financial manipulations have been adopted which it is unnecessary to detail; but on the 29th of October 1890, Her Majesty the Queen was pleased to grant a Royal Charter[1] to the British South Africa Company, which now holds to South and Central Africa a somewhat similar position to

[1] The text of this Charter is so important that it is published, for reference, in the Appendix (A).

that held last century towards Hindostan by the Great East India Company.

The march of the ten thousand, described in such a graphic manner by Xenophon, thrilled the ancient world with admiration. In modern times there has been nothing more deserving of a new Anabasis than the heroic progress of the pioneer force of the British South Africa Company through a roadless country, extending from British Bechuanaland across the Shashi, Nuanetzi and Lundi Rivers, to the great eastern plateau where now the town of Salisbury stands. The expedition comprised 700 carefully-selected Europeans, and 150 native labourers, all fully equipped with the best weapons of precision, accompanied by mountain guns and the electric 'Search' light. They boldly set out under the command of Colonel Pennefather of the Inniskillen Dragoons, and had to march 1000 miles through the country of a most warlike and powerful race of savages, and although a concession had been obtained, it seemed probable that the braves of Lo Bengula would rush with impetuosity to flesh their assegais in the bodies of the invaders.

General Methuen inspected the force at the end of June, and then Major Johnson's

400 pioneers, and four troops of the British South Africa Company's Police, set out on their march along the new track to the Tuli River. Here a letter was received from Lo Bengula, intimating that he would not have a road made, and that if the white impi advanced there would be trouble. At this time, when the coloured boys fled, an opportune contingent of 200 men arrived from Khama. These were invaluable as scouts, divided into five parties, each of which in turn rode first twenty miles or so along the back track of the pioneers, and then circled round the advancing expedition at a distance of from ten to twenty miles. This arrangement made it impossible for the enemy to attack without timely notice, and is one of those lessons which past events in South Africa seem to make it desirable that British generals should study.

B troop, under Captain Hoste, cut the first heavy section of the road, which, beyond the Umzingwan River, included seventeen miles of thick forest, with no water. On the 13th of July they met twenty elephants, but no one dared at any time to fire a shot at game. Every possible precaution was taken. Not only were scouts always out, but while half the men used their axes, the other half on horseback held their comrades' steeds in readiness, and carried their rifles. Every evening the camp was surrounded by a zeriba of thorn trees. When the exhausted men lay down to rest, night was made hideous by the roars of wild beasts. On one occasion Mr Selous tells us a hyena uttered the most unearthly noise that he ever heard. The hideous serenade with which they were entertained stirred sad memories, and almost made him think that an African banshee was forewarning disaster. On 18th July the whole column united, and parallel roads were formed, on which the two-mile procession of waggons advanced. On the 1st of August the Lundi River was arrived at, and then, winding through open forests, they reached the top of a plateau, and beheld thence a sight which gladdened their eyes. As Xenophon's ten thousand cried aloud with transports of delight when they saw the sea, so did the hearts of the pioneers beat with pleasure when they beheld before them the open grassy downs in which the township of Victoria now stands. The real dangers of the journey were over when they passed through Providential Pass.

An ultimatum was now received from Lo

Bengula, ordering Colonel Pennefather to retrace his steps 'unless he was strong enough to go on.' The Matabele king delayed too long, and when he heard that the expedition had reached the open plateau of Mashonaland, he knew that his chance of attack had passed. His position was an extremely difficult one, as during all this time the excitement of the people was extreme, and every preparation for war had to be made. It must be remembered that the old men knew everything about recent Kafir and Zulu wars, and that the memory of their signal defeat by the Boers in 1836 had never been forgotten. Two principal reasons, however, must be quoted to account for the Matabele nation refraining from war. One was the encampment of 500 Bechuanaland Police on the south-western border of Matabeleland, and the other the fact that the whereabouts of our expedition was never known until it reached Mashonaland. On the 1st of September the source of the Umgezi River was reached, where Fort Charter was established, and on the 11th of September 1890 the British flag waved over Fort Salisbury.

Mashonaland was found to be a very sparsely-peopled country. Oft-recurring raids upon the

unwarlike inhabitants had almost completely
depopulated large tracts. As Mr Selous[1] tells
us, in consequence of the never-ceasing attacks
of the fierce Matabele, the high plateau of
Mashonaloud, which at no distant date must
have supported a large native population, once
more became an almost uninhabited wilderness,
as the remnants of the aboriginal tribes who
escaped destruction at the hands of the Zulu
invaders retreated into the broken country
which encircles the plateau to the south and
east. Had it not been for this constant
destruction during the last eighty years there
would be no room to-day for Europeans. As
it is, however, the British South Africa Company has not only effected an occupation
without wronging the natives, but has really
been the means of saving them from continued
and absolute destruction. What is the value
of the country? No man knows it better than
the writer we are now quoting from, and he
assures us that Mashonaland is no longer an
interesting experiment, but a British Colony,
in which it has been proved that European
men and women can thrive. The gold districts
are so rich that each of them will eventually
bear a large population. 'The future of the

[1] *Travel and Adventure in South-East Africa*, p. 345.

vast fields of Mashonaland and Manica seems now so absolutely assured, that it appears odd that doubts should ever have been entertained of their value. . . . Payable reefs have now been proved to a considerable depth in every district. All that is required is the capital necessary to erect quartz-crushing machinery, and carry on the development.'[1]

The pioneers were disbanded, turned their swords into prospecting picks, and having obtained a kingdom, proceeded to search for gold in it. But the summer rains of 1891 were extremely heavy, and caused much sickness and suffering. There was neither adequate protection from the weather nor good food, and the consequences had to be suffered. In addition to the great old workings of the gold-seekers of the time of King Solomon, and their comparatively modern successors of 'Monomotapa' it was soon ascertained that in five districts new gold-bearing formations existed, covering an area 230 miles long by 120 broad, and it was very evident that the British Africa Company had entered into a country which was worth fighting for. Mr A. R. Colquhoun was the first Administrator appointed, and his first difficulties were with the Portuguese. A rapid

[1] Selous's *Travel and Adventure in South-East Africa*, p. 351.

journey was made to Manika, where a treaty had to be entered into with the chief Umtasa, and we are told that on the way up not a vestige of present or past Portuguese occupation was perceptible. The Administrator also tells us that he passed through some of the most charming scenes imaginable, crossing numerous streams of clear, swiftly-flowing water over rocky beds, winding their way amongst perfect wooded mountain scenery, of which one could find its exact counterpart in favoured portions of either Scotland or Wales. When they met Umtasa they found the great chieftain attired in a pair of very old trousers, with a leopard skin slung over his shoulder and a cocked hat on his head. He was preceded by the court jester, who danced round him and cried aloud that his master was the lion who walked by night, before whom the Portuguese and Matabele trembled. After repeated assurances from Umtasa that he had not granted any previous concession, a treaty was signed between the Company and this potentate. The Portuguese connected with the Mozambique Company now cried out that they were defrauded, as they claimed a large tract of country west of Massa Kessi, but although Umtasa admitted that he had accepted presents, he positively denied having given up any portion of his country. Baron de Rezende represented His Most Faithful Majesty, and protested against the presence of our British Africa Company both in Manika and Mashonaland. The fable of the dog in the manger was vividly illustrated, and to carry out this Portuguese policy an armed force of 300 men under Colonel D'Andrada was sent to punish Umtasa. Major Forbes, commanding the British Africa Company's Police, was obliged to request the withdrawal of this force, and, upon a refusal having been returned, proceeded with an escort of twelve men to Umtasa's kraal, and, meeting Baron de Rezende on the threshold, immediately arrested him. The natives rushed to arms, but were too late, as the fort had been already taken by a *coup de main*. Without losing a man, both the place and person of the chief were secured. Great excitement was aroused in Portugal, and, amidst the plaudits of thousands, bands of student volunteers were enrolled and sent off to Beira, at the mouth of the Pungwe River, to drive perfidious Britain from its usurped position. The only result was an attack on a border police post at Umtali, where the Portuguese force was easily repulsed by Captain Heyman and a small number of police. Negotiations were opened in Europe, and on the

11th June 1891 a convention was arranged fixing boundaries. All this, however, is temporary. The sun of Portugal has for ever set in South-Eastern Africa, and the degenerate sons of the heroes of the Lusiad will not be long able to retain territories in which their rule has never been respected.

# CHAPTER XI

*Gazaland—Progress of Events in Mashonaland—Nature and Character of the Country—The Matabele persecute and hunt down the Mashonas — Chartered Company interferes—War with Lo Bengula—Defeat of the Zulu Forces—Death of the King—Conclusion.*

GAZALAND is one of the grandest portions of South-Eastern Africa. Mr Selous, who concluded a treaty with Matoko, paramount chief of the Mabudja, describes it as a magnificent country, possessing every requisite for agriculture or stock-farming. At about 5000 feet above sea level, there are gentle undulating downs, intersected by streams of clear water, and over which are scattered patches of forest. Green, well-watered valleys, interspersed with granite hills, and a cool, delightful and healthy climate. A paradise for the downtrodden, struggling men and women in the gloomy, overcrowded countries of the north of Europe. But this territory is a mere patch and section of the vast empire

now thrown open for the enterprise of the people
of Europe, including much more land than is
comprised in France, Austria and Germany
combined. A commission of South African
farmers, who visited the country to be able to
judge of its nature and character, reported
favourably on a tract of 40,000 square miles
which they had examined. Everywhere they
found traces of agriculture in former ages, but
the peaceful cultivators had been killed or driven
out, and it was necessary that the destroyer
should be destroyed before the arts of peace
were possible. This has now been done, and
the incalculable advantage of doing so can really
only be fully appreciated when we know the
nature and character of the savage tyranny
whose downfall we have to chronicle. The
Company has from the first adopted the policy
of encouraging emigration. Land is given to
settlers on the payment of an annual quit-
rent in advance of £3 per 3000 acres, and
4s. for every additional 200 acres. No single
grant can exceed 6000 acres, and the grantee
must occupy the land himself, or provide
an approved substitute. The Mashonas, reduced in their number though they be, still
cultivate large tracts of country. Descending
from their rocky fastnesses into the fertile plains,

they again produce large crops of cereals as well as rice, and become a happy, contented people, instead of the hunted victims of the most sanguinary tyrants who have ever robbed and murdered in South Africa.

The great pioneer expedition cost the Chartered Company £89,000, and among its results were the formation of a serviceable road, 400 miles long, known as 'Selous Road,' and the erection of forts at Tuli, Victoria, Charter and Salisbury, each of which was manned with a sufficient garrison. Hospitals were established, telegraph lines pushed forward, and arrangements made for the construction of the Cape Colonial Railway to Vryburg in Bechuanaland, afterwards extended to Mafeking.[1] The Barotse king had already granted a mineral and trading concession, which the Company acquired over a country which covers 225,000 square miles, and is reported to be very fertile and healthy, except in the neighbourhood of the Zambesi. This monarch sent two magnificent elephant tusks, each weighing 100 lbs., as a proof of his goodwill, to the directors of the Company.

It is absolutely necessary to notice a fact of considerable significance which has had some-

[1] It is now arranged that the railway is to be continued towards Tati.

thing to do with the perpetual hostility with which the operations of the Company have been regarded, and that is the earnest desire of the Transvaal Boers to obtain Matabeleland, and their natural disappointment at the success of the British Africa Company. For several years a section of the Transvaal farmers cherished a scheme for occupying Matabeleland and Mashonaland, in which they would have erected a new state. Indeed, overtures were several times made by them to Lo Bengula, which he never entertained; and both in 1890 and 1891 information was received that a force would leave the Transvaal with the object of seizing a part of the south-eastern section of Matabeleland. Prompt measures, taken both by the High Commissioner and the Company, prevented this calamity. Representations were successfully made to President Kruger, and the police force was considerably increased. It will thus be seen that if the British Empire's forward policy in Africa is a wise one, it was absolutely necessary to be in advance of the Boers of the Transvaal in securing territories and rights in the countries which extend between the Zambesi and Limpopo Rivers.

The first Administrator of Mashonaland was Mr A. R. Colquhoun, who had accompanied the pioneer expedition, and who subsequently was the intermediary in obtaining large concessions. In consequence of failing health he was succeeded towards the end of 1891 by Dr L. S. Jameson, whose experience in dealing with natives, and whose popularity with the community soon pointed him out as a beau ideal Governor. It would be tiresome to enter into the details connected with the establishment of a new country. The wet season and the want of transport were soon seen to be the principal obstacles to progress. Numbers of good reefs were discovered, but how was it possible to transport heavy machinery to them? The Beira line was therefore undertaken, as a very narrow guage railway, to take goods from an excellent port at the mouth of the Pungwe River through the fly country to Salisbury. This will be extended still further, so that the programme of the Chartered Company is to have a cheap railway from Beira to Buluwayo, and an extension of the Cape Colonial line from Mafeking *via* Tati to the same point. The distinction between Mashonaland, with Salisbury as its principal town, and Matabeleland, where the new town of Buluwayo has been established, should be put an end to, and the country be known under one title as 'Rhodesia,' which, although large, is only a province or section of the immense territories of the Company stretching northward almost to the great lakes.

Missions to various chiefs north of the Zambesi have been successfully sent out from time to time, and reports concerning new kingdoms placed under our sphere of influence are extremely interesting. Mr Joseph Thomson, of Masailand fame, states that in course of performing his duty to the Company he travelled a distance of 1250 miles—from Katakota to Lake Nyassa—and of this distance over 900 miles represented entirely new country. Treaties concluded with various chiefs referred almost exclusively to the Loangwa Kafue Plateau, which practically includes an area of about 40,000 square miles, extending between latitudes 12° and 15° S., and longitudes 28° and 31° E. The true value of this country lies in its productiveness, as more than three-fourths of its territory consists of capital agricultural and pastoral land. 'Indeed,' we are told, 'for such an extent of country, its high average value is quite exceptional for Africa, so much of which is either hopelessly swampy or as hopelessly arid and sterile. Neither the one nor the other of these drawbacks prevail in even a minor degree over the whole of these favoured uplands. . . . A glance at the map will show the remarkable number of perennial streams and rivers which water this favoured region.' Here are thousands of square miles fit for the planter, and over the cool uplands countless herds of cattle and flocks of sheep could be successfully reared. The climate is deliciously cool and exceptionally healthy. As the geology of this region is closely identical with that of Mashonaland, it is not surprising that Mr Thomson should say that it seemed to him the promise of gold was most marked. What a charming part of the world to live in! Standing on a crest of the highest ridge, looking westward, you see mapped out before you the plateau or basin of Milangi, with its rolling hills of grassy sward, its clearly-defined belts of dark green forest, and its numerous ravines or rivulets all shaping their course towards the principal valley of the plateau, through which the Lutshenga, the main stream, flows. Still looking towards the west, there are on the right the peaks of the mountain rising directly from the valley of the Lutshenga, which runs parallel with its southern base. In the distance, across the tableland, is the isolated Chambi range, while to the front and on the left rolling grassy hills, capped with rugged cliffs of granite, encircle the plateau.[1] The British South Africa Company opens this country to the over-populated countries of the old world, and this alone should be enough to establish its claim to gratitude and recognition. There is abundance of room both for the present inhabitants and the new-comers, and anything more absurd than the contention that we are injuring native interests it is impossible to conceive. No doubt Divine Providence is now opening up vast regions where new homes will yet be found for thousands. Certain it is but for the fact that gold exists extensively in Matabeleland the Mashonas would continue downtrodden, plundered and massacred, while the introduction of Christianity among the fierce Zulus would remain impossible.

The work of the British South Africa Company has added about 750,000 square miles to the British Empire, and laid the foundation of a valuable colony. To use their own words, their 'policy has been to secure the high tableland which extends throughout the centre of South Africa from the Karoo Desert northwards, for it is here that a white population can thrive, and temperate, as well as many tropical, plants can be grown.' This tableland extends

[1] See the excellent description of this country from the pen of Mr Thomson, published in the Report of the British South Africa Company for 1889-92.

through Matabeleland, and beyond the Zambesi, up to the confines of the Congo Free State. Treaties have been made with Gunyunhena, who claimed to divide with Lo Bengula all the country between the Zambesi and the Vaal, and also with the chief of the Barotse, whose territory extends to the Portuguese province of Angola. The African Lake Company has been taken over, and their property confirmed, so that the development of Nyassaland is now made possible. The more that is known about these regions the more they will be appreciated.

In somewhat of a spirit of prophecy we are told by a Scotsman, who writes from Salisbury, and is quoted by the Duke of Fife at the meeting of the Company, held in December 1893, that 'As soon as the Matabele are settled you will see the country go ahead. Labour will become certain and steady, as the natives will have nothing to dread. The mining machinery will be set going; farming will proceed, and cattle will be reared without the fear of their being raided on. . . . I would not be surprised to see two or three Johannesburgs appear before many years are over. . . . Thousands of our countrymen who are too crowded here will take advantage of the enormous space, the healthful climate, and the immense resources which this territory offers to those who will go in and possess the land.'

And now it is necessary to pay special attention to the last important events in the history of the expansion of Southern Africa. For some time prior to July 14, 1893, more than 5000 Matabeles had been raiding in the Victoria district of the Chartered Company's territory, killing Mashonas in the employ of Europeans under the eyes of their masters, and also burning huts and stores, as well as stealing cattle on farms occupied by Europeans. The Administrator hastened from Salisbury to Victoria, and at once sent for the head Indunas of the Matabele Impi, who were most insolent. They were then told by Dr Jameson that he would drive them out if they had not commenced to go within one hour. One hour and forty minutes were then actually allowed to transpire, and then Captain Lendi, R.A.,[1] magistrate of the Victoria District, received instructions to follow the Impi with thirty-

[1] Anything more absurd or unjust than the charges made against the British authorities in South Africa at this time can scarcely be imagined. A host of witnesses unexceptionable in character prove this. For instance, Father Barthelemy, S.J., living at this time at Victoria, was perfectly impartial, and utterly unconnected with any schemes of aggrandisement. He was one of those Europeans whose counsel was asked, and he

eight mounted men, and if they had not then commenced a retreat to fire upon them. This command was absolutely required by the circumstances. The party went forth, and found the Matabeles, so far from beginning to retire from the country, absolutely continuing their outrages, by besieging Magomela's kraal, distant only four miles from Victoria. As soon as the Matabele saw the advanced guard of the mounted troop they opened fire, and this was of course returned, and with such effect that the enemy fled, and forty of them were killed, including the most impertinent of the Indunas. The main body of the Matabele then thought fit to cross the border, and Dr Jameson wired to Lo Bengula, demanding the infliction of punishment on the Indunas, and compensation for damages. He also informed the king that the white people could not give up Mashona women and children to be slaughtered when they had claimed their protection, but if they had done wrong they could be punished on conviction before a magistrate. The king's reply at first was pacific, but when his people

testifies that, so far from Captain Lendi being sanguinary, his fault was that he was rather too much inclined to leniency. Nothing was done either cruelly or unjustly; on the contrary, the only possible course was pursued for the safety of the people under the Government and the honour of the nation it represented.

reported the skirmish then his tone changed, and he demanded the unconditional surrender of Mashona men, women and children. These he evidently looked upon as his property, to be killed or placed in slavery. Of course, the High Commissioner could not accede, and hence the war.

Everyone acquainted with the history and character of the Matabele warriors knew well that, if we had allowed them to kill Mashonas, the turn of Europeans would have come next. The people who had settled in the country under the Queen's Charter were entitled to protection, and they, as well, indeed, as the Government, were perfectly aware that the time had now come for vigorous and instantaneous action. Nothing, however, should or could be done without the sanction of the Imperial Government. Defence columns were organised, 750 horses purchased, and the best routes into Matabeleland surveyed. On the 25th of September two men of Captain White's patrol were fired on near the border. From native intelligence, corroborated by Mr Calenbrander's reports, it was learned that the Matabele were advancing in great force in two divisions, and on the 5th of October a patrol of the Imperial force, styled the British

Bechuanaland Police, was fired on in the Protectorate, south of the Shashi River. Under these circumstances, the High Commissioner felt it to be his duty to telegraph his sanction of a general forward movement into Matabeleland.

The force collected included the Salisbury column, under Major Forbes, of 269 Europeans, 106 armed coolies and Cape-boys, 258 horses, 2 Maxim guns, 1 'Nordenfeldt,' 1 'Gardner,' and 18 waggons; the Victoria column, under Major Alan Wilson, of 397 Europeans, 60 armed Cape-boys, 272 horses, 3 Maxims, 1 'Hotchkiss,' 1 seven-pounder, also sky-rockets, etc., 330,000 rounds of ammunition for Martini and machine guns, and 1800 shells of all sorts; Major Raaff's rangers of 235 men and 191 horses, with 70,000 rounds of Martini. The officers and men of the three columns, including armed natives, numbered 1067. One thousand men, it may be said, went forth to conquer one of the most sanguinary and powerful people of the southern portion of the continent, and did it. Did it in an extraordinarily short space of time, as they acted under skilful officers, with thorough knowledge both of the people and of the country—without delay, and with vigour and celerity. It must be added that this force was subsequently augmented on its march by a native contingent of Mashonas over 1200 strong, but these, although useful as scouts and in clearing the bush, were not of much account in actual fighting. Major Willoughby was chief in command, and His Honour the Administrator, Dr Jameson, undertook personal superintendence and supreme control of the advance on Buluwayo, as well as of the operations against the Matabele.

As soon as the British force commenced to advance, seven Matabele regiments which had taken the field began to retreat on the Changani River. Two powerful Makalaka chiefs sent propitiatory presents, and it thus became evident that decisive and rapid action had a most excellent effect. Carefulness is always shown by good leaders, who never undervalue the enemy, nor give him an unnecessary opportunity. The native contingents were distributed in front and rear, as well as on both flanks, to a radius of five or six miles, but when the columns got into touch with the retreating Matabele regiments European scouts had to be depended on, as our native allies showed a great disinclination to go much in advance. The Shashi River was the rubicon of the expedition, and after crossing it Mashonaland was left behind, and the invasion of Matabeleland commenced. Two miles beyond the Umgezi River, bush country (chiefly Magondi Forest) ended, and a high plateau with open country was reached. On the 15th of October the scouts were attacked by 2000 Matabele, who subsequently retired and allowed a considerable number of cattle to be captured. The chief guide of the expedition, named Manyezi, belonged to a portion of the Matabele which had been practically annihilated by Lo Bengula. Revenge, therefore, incited him to lead destroying bands against his people's destroyer.

On the 21st of October, Dr Jameson and Major Willoughby, accompanied by Major Wilson with 100 mounted men and two Maxims, proceeded to attack the great kraal of the Insukamini Regiment, which was situated on a rising and fairly open ground half a mile from the Gwelo River. The Insuka Regiment, close at hand, looking on from the thick bush, was afraid to attack, and the kraal itself was undefended. So all that could be done was to burn the huts, and return to the main column. A forest was then penetrated, in which the Matabele had intended to make an attack; but, fortunately, they had received wrong information about our line of march, and, therefore, did not make the attempt. Sixty Mashona women were soon afterwards recaptured, and about 1000 head of cattle and a large number of sheep and goats secured. At last, between two tributaries of the Changani River, the enemy attacked by opening a continuous and steady fire on all sides with Martini rifles and muzzle-loaders. The machine guns were brought into play, and, unfortunately, a number of the native contingent in running away got into their fire and were killed. The enemy's first attack was chiefly directed against the right and rear of the Salisbury laager and rear faces of the Victoria laager. The Matabele were so near that their shouts of encouragement to each other could be plainly heard, and in some instances they advanced within eighty yards of the entrenchments. For twenty minutes the machine guns let havoc loose among them, and the bravest of the brave savages of Lo Bengula's army were forced to retire. Two troops then advanced to clear the bush under Captains Henny and Spreckley, but were forced to retreat, and by their presence in the field prevented the Maxims firing on masses of the enemy. Then came the second attack, when daylight rendered it more difficult, and previous repulses made it less determined. At this time Matabele reinforcements collected together in a large body on an eminence, which was immediately shelled by a seven-pounder gun. The second shell caused the enemy to scatter, upon which Captains Fitzgerald and Bastard swept the ground with their mounted men. The enemy were driven back across the stream, and a 'Hotchkiss' gun brought to bear on them did good execution. The Maxims and a seven-pounder were now advanced, and poured shell into the enemy; and then the battle was completely over, and the Matabele nation had to recognise a conqueror. Six thousand of their best troops were in the engagement, and out of that number 600 were killed. Our losses comprised twenty-two killed and thirty-eight wounded. They had intended to attack at 10 p.m., but postponed the movement until four in the morning on account of three rockets being sent up at 8 p.m. to acquaint a belated patrol with the neighbourhood of the camp. These excited their amazement and alarm at the strange power of the European magicians, and frightened them into a delay which did not improve their chances of success.

Various attacks of the enemy *en route* were repulsed. Captain Williams unfortunately lost his life in consequence of his horse bolting into the ranks of the enemy. Skirmishes and cattle captures took place; and at last, as the Chartered Company's forces neared Buluwayo, everything pointed to a decisive engagement being close at hand. It came at last, very early in the afternoon of the 31st October, when the best regiment of the Matabele hurled itself against the entrenched or laagered columns. The enemy were brave, but would have fared better if they had attacked us on the march, and trusted to their assegais shortened and used as stabbing swords rather than to weapons with which comparatively few of them were acquainted. The main attack was made by the famous Umbezu and Ingubu cohorts, which occupied a front of about three-quarters of a mile. Major Willoughby declares that he could not but admire the pluck of these men, 'which was simply splendid,' and he doubts whether any European troops would have stood as long as they did the terrific and well-directed fire of the most deadly weapons of destruction yet invented. An hour of carnage ensued, during which the machine-guns played upon the enemy, and then they began to retreat after a loss of nearly 1000 killed and wounded. The latter were borne from the field by the Matabele, who made good their retreat by taking advantage of the bushy country in the neighbourhood. The casualties on the side of the Chartered Company's forces were strangely small, comprising only four killed and a few wounded, bearing testimony to the enormous advantages of an entrenched position defended by artillery. It must be admitted that the Matabele were badly commanded throughout. The king's orders were to attack the invaders on the march, and not when laagered; and on the occasion of this last and greatest battle their deficiency in intelligence was as great as their want of tactical skill. They absolutely did not know that their enemy was laagered, and believed that with an overwhelming force they could easily succeed in mastering a handful of men, and carry them off as slaves.

On the 3d of November, at 7.30 a.m., a loud report rent the air, and huge columns of smoke were observed to rise from Buluwayo, where 80,000 rounds of Martini-Henry ammunition and 2500 pounds of gunpowder were blown up by the panic-stricken inhabitants, from whom their king had fled, and who knew that the dreaded white magicians were close at hand. The machine guns were now brought to bear upon the bush, which was shelled, and shortly afterwards the place of Lo Bengula, deserted and in flames, was entered by the conquering expedition. This last and most unfortunate ruler of the Matabele was now a wretched fugitive flying to the northward under the protection of the scattered remnants of his army.

The chief Gambo had gone south with 4000 men to oppose Colonel Goold Adams, who commanded the British Bechuanaland Police. These powerful reinforcements were detained on the march, and had to repel a sharp attack made by the Matabele forces sent to intercept them. On this occasion (2d November) the column of Colonel Goold Adams was partially laagered, but some of the waggons were inspanned ready to start when the Matabele charged in great numbers, and succeeded in capturing a waggon, which they burnt. Mr Selous, who was acting as guide, galloped back in advance of a mounted force sent to protect the waggons, and, while engaging the enemy, was slightly wounded. All the other waggons succeeded in reaching the laager, and, after a sharp, short contest, the enemy was routed and pursued for some distance, losing about 100 men. Two Europeans were killed, and five wounded. Two days afterwards, Khama and all his natives turned back on the plea that he feared smallpox, then prevalent in the district, would spread among his men. In this manner the reinforcements were reduced to 400 men when they reached Buluwayo.

Messages were sent to the king, but the ambassadors were treated roughly, and narrowly escaped with their lives. They were threatened and prodded with assegais while discussions proceeded as to whether they should be maimed or killed. Some of the Indunas and old men had to protect them from the ferocious Matabele youths, who still cried out for war. The king desired to surrender, and said so, but nothing was done, although it subsequently transpired that he sent messengers with money, which was stolen by two men of the police, who were afterwards discovered and punished. For the speedy pacification of the country a force was at once despatched, consisting of 300 mounted men with four Maxims and one seven-pounder, under the command of Major Forbes and Captain Raaff,

C.M.G. These officers lost no time in starting, and hoped by two night marches and halting during the day to arrive unexpectedly at the place where the king was supposed to be—about forty-two miles from Buluwayo. Unfortunately, only three days' supplies were taken, which caused the patrol to turn back when near their destination, and entailed protracted operations which extended over a month. If it had gone smartly on, without delay or hesitation, the king would have been found in fairly open country, twenty-four miles down the Bubye River, and the subsequent march to the Changani through thick bush country avoided. At this time the Umbezu regiment was in the bush waiting for an opportunity to surrender, but numbers of turbulent Matabele still ranged the country, thirty of whom drove the native contingent men in, and, within full sight of the camp, boldly seized on 1000 cattle. Most of these were recaptured, and several of the raiders shot. New orders now were issued for the patrol to march on Sheloh, where reinforcements and waggons with supplies would meet them. A re-arranged force left that place on the 25th of November, consisting of 165 mounted and 105 dismounted men, 4

Maxims, a 'Hotchkiss' gun, and 5 waggons carrying reserves of ammunition—the balance of the force, consisting of 280 men, with the seven-pounder returned to Buluwayo. Heavy rains came on, and so impeded the progress of the patrol that Major Forbes subdivided his force, and determined to push on without waggons. Up to the 2d of December no incident of any importance occurred, and from intelligence received from various sources it was believed that the king had only a few men with him. On the next day, the hut of the king was captured, from which he had only fled that morning. Major Wilson and eighteen men were immediately sent forward along the spoor to reconnoitre, and they were instructed to return by sundown. Unfortunately large numbers of broken regiments had massed together at this point, and a portion of our divided force, which had an inadequate supply of ammunition, fell victims. Major Wilson sent for reinforcements, but the main body was itself in terrible straits, and could only send twenty men. Major Wilson went up to the king's waggon, from which he had fled on horseback, and while slowly retreating found himself surrounded by an overwhelming force of Matabele warriors. Here were thirty-three officers and men with hundreds of fierce savages howling for their blood, and in the annals of no nation can we find a finer example of steady courage and devotion than was exhibited on this occasion. It was while retreating that Burnham Ingram and Gooding were sent off to the main body for reinforcements. Finding themselves completely surrounded, Major Wilson's party formed a ring of their horses, and made their last stand on the king's waggon spoor. There they fought for hours, until their ammunition was expended, while the dead bodies of their horses were formed into barricades. Twice were the enemy driven off by these heroes, but here endurance and courage were in vain. The last cartridge was at last expended, and then —but not till then—did the Matabele warriors advance and dare to stab their gallant opponents to death. Each of the party killed at least ten of the enemy, so that literally a fence of corpses piled one upon the other lay around. Although the bodies of the white men were stripped and mutilated, the natives were struck with admiration at the manner in which they had not only fought, but died. Without a struggle or a murmur they submitted to their doom, tenderly assisting their companions to the last—some of the men even stripping themselves of their shirts to make bandages for the wounded.

The main body of the patrol under Major Forbes was placed in terrible difficulties, in the midst of heavy rains, with swollen rivers to cross, and an overwhelming force of the enemy around them. Two mounted messengers were sent to Dr Jameson at Buluwayo to report events and apply for assistance. A large force was immediately sent out, which the Administrator accompanied, and strong patrols were despatched in various directions. In a few days time the relief column, with Mr Selous, joined the retreating party under Major Forbes, and found that the men had suffered severe hardships, having been compelled to eat their own horses, but, nevertheless, with the exception of five wounded men, were all doing well and able to ride. Mr Rhodes and Mr Sawyer, military secretary to the High Commissioner, both accompanied the relief party.

The Matabele now commenced to come in and make submission. By the end of December 1893 large numbers of natives, including many of the principal Indunas, had not only declared in favour of the new Government, but had settled down on their lands, and, turning their swords into ploughshares, commenced to cultivate them. No fewer than 10,000 assegais, and more than 1000 guns and rifles were given up. The new rule was a blessed one of peace and safety as compared with the former sanguinary tyranny, under which neither life nor property was at any time safe. Where is the native tribe, long under the British flag in Southern Africa, which, if it had its choice, would go back to the murders and robberies of the ancient regime, where witchcraft was religion and the chief's will law? The Mashonas are no longer more cruelly treated than the beasts of the field, and under a Government where security of life and property exists, come down from their fastnesses and cultivate the fruitful fields so long left desolate. Enormous tracts of excellent country, great mines of wealth, the treasures of nature, are opened up to the world, and through the golden gates of mineral discovery, civilisation, peace and prosperity now enter a land which was constantly the scene of bloodshed and superstition.

The last of the Matabele kings must have terribly felt the awful reverse of fortune which reduced him from supreme power to that of a hunted fugitive. It was difficult to open up communications with Lo Bengula, for although Messrs Tainton, Riley and Dawson volunteered to go, no Indunas could be found willing to accompany them. They were all afraid to face the man whose word had meant life or death. The principal Matabele leaders came in one after another and surrendered. At last news arrived from Mjan, giving full particulars of the death of the king at a place within forty miles of the Zambesi. One man only, the Induna Bosumidan, was present when this formerly powerful ruler breathed his last, and it is very possible that his only companion put him to death. Like Cato he may have asked his friend to kill him, but whether suicide or murder effected the object remains a mystery. Probably, under the circumstances, one or other of these two caused his death rather than natural illness. Thus passed away the last of the sanguinary tyrants, whose system of rule had hitherto prevented the possibility of Christianity and of civilisation entering Matabeleland.

An agreement between Her Majesty's Government and the British South Africa Company relative to Matabele and Mashonaland was signed on the 23d of May 1894, and is so important that it is printed in the Appendix (B). Under this the amplest powers and advantages are secured to the British Africa Company.

Many facts of history, like many oil paintings, require to be looked at from some distance in order to be seen aright. A time is not far distant when Englishmen will feel surprised at the strange calumnies which accompanied the first years of the British Chartered Company's efforts and rule in Southern Africa. The High Commissioner, Sir Henry Loch, as well as Mr Rhodes and those associated with him, will then perhaps receive that meed of praise and of gratitude which their services merit. A great page in the history of British enterprise is now being written. We have endeavoured to chronicle the events connected with the infancy and early youth of Southern Africa, and now that manhood seems to be at hand, it is very desirable to consider well the expansion which has taken place, as we know that 'The child is father to the man.' A new era has certainly dawned, and it behoves the people of Europe to weigh well the situation, and to take early advantage of the great opportunities now placed within their reach.

The task of sketching briefly the history of the expansion of Southern Africa from the earliest period to the present time concludes with the last great events connected with the territory of the British Africa Company between the Limpopo and Zambesi Rivers. In the South African Republic we see at present a justly discontented people, bearing the principal financial burdens of the State, but condemned by the oligarchy which controls the Government to be excluded from participation in the franchise, as well as exposed to oppressive exactions and unjust monopolies. In the Orange Free State there is a happy, well-governed people, while Natal is wisely ruled under its new system of responsible government. Strange to say the only customs union which exists is between the Cape Colony, the Orange Free State, Bechuanaland and Basutoland, but a time must come when, for mutual interests, all the civilised states south of the Zambesi will unite in a federation under which they will all enjoy free trade with each other, and mutually agreed-upon customs, postal, telegraphic and railway tariffs. The line from Delagoa Bay to Johannesburg is fast attaining completion, and then it will be possible to travel by railway from that port to Capetown, a distance of more than 1500 miles. New railways are projected, mining enterprise is carried on in a very extensive and successful manner. On the whole, it seems that South Africa, awakened to real life in the latter portion of the nineteenth century, is only now really beginning its national life.

# APPENDIX (A).

CHARTER OF THE BRITISH SOUTH AFRICA COMPANY.

Victoria, by the Grace of God, of the United Kingdom of Great Britain and Ireland, Queen, Defender of the Faith,—

To all to whom these presents shall come, Greeting :

WHEREAS a Humble Petition has been presented to us in our Council by the Most Noble James, Duke of Abercorn, Companion of the Most Honourable Order of the Bath ; the Most Noble Alexander William George, Duke of Fife, Knight of the Most Ancient and Most Noble Order of the Thistle, Privy Councillor ; the Right Honourable Edric Frederick, Lord Gifford, V.C. ; Cecil John Rhodes, of Kimberley, in the Cape Colony, Member of the Executive Council and of the House of Assembly of the Colony of the Cape of Good Hope ; Alfred Beit, of 29 Holburn

Viaduct, London, Merchant; Albert Henry George Grey, of Howick, Northumberland, Esquire; and George Cawston, of 18 Lennox Gardens, London, Esquire, Barrister-at-Law.

And whereas the said Petition states amongst other things :—

> That the Petitioners and others are associated for the purpose of forming a Company or Association, to be incorporated, if to us should seem fit, for the objects in the said Petition set forth, under the corporate name of The British South Africa Company :
>
> That the existence of a powerful British Company, controlled by those of our subjects in whom we have confidence, and having its principal field of operations in that region of South Africa lying to the north of Bechuanaland and to the west of Portuguese East Africa, would be advantageous to the commercial and other interests of our subjects in the United Kingdom and in our Colonies :
>
> That the Petitioners desire to carry into effect divers concessions and agreements which have been made by certain of

## Appendix

the chiefs and tribes inhabiting the said region, and such other concessions, agreements, grants and treaties as the Petitioners may hereafter obtain within the said region or elsewhere in Africa, with the view of promoting trade, commerce, civilisation and good government (including the regulation of liquor traffic with the natives) in the territories which are or may be comprised or referred to in such concessions agreements grants, and treaties as aforesaid :

That the Petitioners believe that if the said concessions, agreements, grants and treaties can be carried into effect, the condition of the natives inhabiting the said territories will be materially improved, and their civilisation advanced. and an organisation established which will tend to the suppression of the slave trade in the said territories, and to the opening up of the said territories to the immigration of Europeans, and to the lawful trade and commerce of our subjects and of other nations :

That the success of the enterprise in which the Petitioners are engaged would be greatly advanced if it should seem fit to us to grant them our Royal Charter of incorporation as a British Company under the said name or title, or such other name or title, and with such powers, as to us may seem fit for the purpose of more effectually carrying into effect the objects aforesaid :

That large sums of money have been subscribed for the purposes of the intended Company by the Petitioners and others, who are prepared also to subscribe or to procure such further sums as may hereafter be found requisite for the development of the said enterprise, in the event of our being pleased to grant to them our Royal Charter of incorporation as aforesaid :

Now therefore we, having taken the said Petition into our royal consideration in our Council, and being satisfied that the intentions of the Petitioners are praiseworthy and deserve encouragement, and that the enterprise in the Petition described may be productive of the benefits set forth therein, by our prerogative royal and of our special grace, certain knowledge and mere motion, have constituted, erected and

## Appendix

incorporated and by this, our charter, for us and our heirs and royal successors, do constitute, erect and incorporate into one body, politic and corporate, by the name of The British South Africa Company, the said James, Duke of Abercorn; Alexander William George, Duke of Fife; Edric Frederick, Lord Gifford; Cecil John Rhodes; Alfred Beit; Albert Henry George Grey and George Cawston, and such other persons and such bodies as from time to time become and are members of the body, politic and corporate, by these presents, constituted, erected and incorporated, with perpetual succession and a common seal, with power to break, alter or renew the same at discretion, and with the further authorities, powers and privileges conferred, and subject to the conditions imposed by this, our charter: And we do hereby accordingly will, ordain, give, grant, constitute, appoint and declare, as follows (that is to say):—

1. The principal field of the operations of the British South Africa Company (in this, our charter, referred to as 'the Company') shall be the region of South Africa lying immediately to the north of British Bechuanaland, and to the north and west of the South

African Republic, and to the west of the Portuguese dominions.

2. The Company is hereby authorised and empowered to hold, use and retain, for the purposes of the Company and on the terms of this, our charter, the full benefit of the concessions and agreements made as aforesaid, so far as they are valid, or any of them, and all interest, authorities and powers comprised or referred to in the said concessions and agreements. Provided always that nothing herein contained shall prejudice or affect any other valid and subsisting concessions or agreements which may have been made by any of the chiefs or tribes aforesaid]; and, in particular, nothing herein contained shall prejudice or affect certain concessions granted in and subsequent to the year 1880 relating to the territory usually known as the district of Tati; nor shall anything herein contained be construed as giving any jurisdiction, administrative or otherwise, within the said district of the Tati, the limits of which district are as follows, viz., from the place where the Shasi River rises to its junction with the Tati and Ramaquaban Rivers, thence along the Ramaquaban River to where it rises, and thence along the watersheds of those rivers.

3. The Company is hereby further authorised and empowered, subject to the approval of one of our principal Secretaries of State (herein referred to as 'our Secretary of State'), from time to time, to acquire by any concession, agreement, grant or treaty, all or any rights, interests, authorities, jurisdictions and powers of any kind or nature whatever, including powers necessary for the purposes of government and the preservation of public order in or for the protection of territories, lands or property comprised or referred to in the concessions and agreements made as aforesaid, or affecting other territories, lands or property in Africa, or the inhabitants thereof, and to hold, use and exercise such territories, lands, property, rights, interests, authorities, jurisdictions and powers respectively for the purpose of the Company, and on the terms of this, our charter.

4. Provided that no powers of government or administration shall be exercised under or in relation to any such last-mentioned concession, agreement, grant or treaty, until a copy of such concession, agreement, grant or treaty, in such form and with such maps or particulars as our Secretary of State approves verified

as he requires, has been transmitted to him, and he has signified his approval thereof, either absolutely or subject to any conditions or reservations; and provided also that no rights, interests, authorities, jurisdictions or powers of any description shall be acquired by the Company within the said district of the Tati as hereinbefore described, without the previous consent in writing of the owners for the time being of the concessions above referred to relating to the said district, and the approval of our Secretary of State.

5. The Company shall be bound by, and shall fulfil, all and singular the stipulations on its part contained in any such concession, agreement, grant or treaty as aforesaid, subject to any subsequent agreement affecting those stipulations approved by our Secretary of State.

6. The Company shall always be and remain British in character and domicile, and shall have its principal office in Great Britain, and the Company's principal representative in South Africa, and the directors shall always be natural born British subjects, or persons who have been naturalised as British subjects by or under an Act of Parliament of our United Kingdom; but this article shall not disqualify

any person nominated a director by this, our charter, or any person whose election as a director shall have been approved by our Secretary of State, from acting in that capacity.

7. In case at any time any difference arises between any chief or tribe inhabiting any of the territories aforesaid and the Company, that difference shall, if our Secretary of State so require, be submitted by the Company to him for his decision, and the Company shall act in accordance with such decision.

8 If at any time our Secretary of State thinks fit to dissent from or object to any of the dealings of the Company with any foreign power, and to make known to the Company any suggestion founded on that dissent or objection, the Company shall act in accordance with such suggestion.

9 If at any time our Secretary of State thinks fit to object to the exercise by the Company of any authority, power or right within any part of the territories aforesaid, on the ground of there being an adverse claim to or in respect of that part, the Company shall defer to that objection until such time as any such claim has been withdrawn, or finally dealt with or settled by our Secretary of State.

10. The Company shall to the best of its ability preserve peace and order in such ways and manners as it shall consider necessary, and may with that object make ordinances (to be approved by our Secretary of State), and may establish and maintain a force of police.

11. The Company shall to the best of its ability discourage, and, so far as may be practicable, abolish by degrees, any system of slave trade or domestic servitude in the territories aforesaid.

12. The Company shall regulate the trafic in spirits and other intoxicating liquors within the territories aforesaid, so as, as far as practicable, to prevent the sale of any spirits or other intoxicating liquor to any natives.

13. The Company as such, or its officers as such, shall not in any way interfere with he religion of any class or tribe of the peoples of the territories aforesaid, or of any of the inhabitants thereof, except so far as may be necessary in the interests of humanity, and all forms of religious worship or religious orlinances may be exercised within the said teritories, and no hindrance shall be offered thereto except as aforesaid.

14. In the administration of justice to the said peoples or inhabitants, careful regard shall always be had to the customs and laws of the class or tribe or nation to which the parties respectively belong, especially with respect to the holding, possession, transfer and disposition of lands and goods, and testate or intestate succession thereto, and marriage, divorce and legitimacy, and other rights of property and personal rights, but subject to any British laws which may be in force in any of the territories aforesaid, and applicable to the peoples or inhabitants thereof.

15. If at any time our Secretary of State thinks fit to dissent from or object to any part of the proceedings or system of the Company relative to the peoples of the territories aforesaid, or to any of the inhabitants thereof, in respect of slavery or religion, or the administration of justice, or any other matter, he shall make known to the Company his dissent or objection, and the Company shall act in accordance with his directions duly signified.

16. In the event of the Company acquiring any harbour or harbours, the Company shall freely afford all facilities for or to our ships therein without payment, except reasonable

charges for work done or services rendered, or materials or things supplied.

17. The Company shall furnish annually to our Secretary of State, as soon as conveniently may be after the close of the financial year, accounts of its expenditure for administrative purposes, and of all sums received by it by way of public revenue, as distinguished from its commercial profits, during the financial year, together with a report as to its public proceedings and the condition of the territories within the sphere of its operations. The Company shall also on or before the commencement of each financial year furnish to our Secretary of State an estimate of its expenditure for administrative purposes, and of its public revenue (as above defined) for the ensuing year. The Company shall, in addition, from time to time, furnish to our Secretary of State any reports, accounts or information with which he may require to be furnished.

18. The several officers of the Company shall, subject to the rules of official subordination and to any regulations that may be agreed upon, communicate freely with our High Commissioner in South Africa, and any others our officers, who may be stationed within any of

*Appendix* 251

the territories aforesaid, and shall pay due regard to any requirements, suggestions or requests which the said High Commissioner or other officers shall make to them or any of them, and the Company shall be bound to enforce the observance of this article.

19. The Company may hoist and use on its buildings and elsewhere in the territories aforesaid, and on its vessels, such distinctive flag, indicating the British character of the Company, as our Secretary of State and the Lords Commissioners of the Admiralty shall from time to time approve.

20. Nothing in this, our charter, shall be deemed to authorise the Company to set up or grant any monopoly of trade, provided that the establishment of, or the grant of, concessions for banks, railways, tramways, docks, telegraphs, waterworks, or other similar undertakings, or the establishment of any system of patent or copyright approved by our Secretary of State, shall not be deemed monopolies for this purpose. The Company shall not either directly or indirectly hinder any company or persons who now are, or hereafter may be, lawfully and peaceably carrying on any business, concern or venture within the said district of the Tati

hereinbefore described, but shall, by permitting and facilitating transit, by every lawful means, to and from the district of the Tati, across its own territories, or where it has jurisdiction in that behalf, and by all other reasonable and lawful means, encourage, assist and protect all British subjects who now are, or hereafter may be, lawfully and peaceably engaged in the prosecution of a lawful enterprise within the said district of the Tati.

21. For the preservation of elephants and other game, the Company may make such regulations and (notwithstanding anything hereinbefore contained) may impose such licence duties on the killing or taking of elephants or other game as they may see fit: Provided that nothing in such regulations shall extend to diminish or interfere with any hunting rights which may have been or may hereafter be reserved to any native chiefs or tribes by treaty, save so far as any such regulations may relate to the establishment and enforcement of a close season.

22. The Company shall be subject to, and shall perform and undertake all the obligations contained in or undertaken by ourselves, under any treaty, agreement or arrangement between

*Appendix* 253

ourselves and any other State or Power, whether already made or hereafter to be made. In all matters relating to the observance of this article, or to the exercise within the Company's territories for the time being of any jurisdiction exerciseable by us under the Foreign Jurisdiction Acts, the Company shall conform to and observe and carry out all such directions as may from time to time be given in that behalf by our Secretary of State, and the Company shall appoint all necessary officers to perform such duties, and shall provide such courts and other requisites as may from time to time be necessary for the administration of justice.

23. The original share capital of the Company shall be £1,000,000, divided into 1,000,000 shares of £1 each.

24. The Company is hereby further specially authorised and empowered for the purposes of this, our charter, from time to time—

> (1.) To issue shares of different classes or descriptions, to increase the share capital of the Company, and to borrow moneys by debentures or other obligations.

(2.) To acquire and hold, and to charter or otherwise deal with steam vessels and other vessels.

(3.) To establish or authorise banking companies and other companies, and undertakings or associations of every description, for purposes consistent with the provisions of this, our charter.

(4.) To make and maintain roads, railways, telegraphs, harbours, and any other works which may tend to the development or improvement of the territories of the Company.

(5.) To carry on mining and other industries, and to make concessions of mining, forestal or other rights.

(6.) To improve, develop, clear, plant, irrigate and cultivate any lands included within the territories of the Company.

(7.) To settle any such territories and lands as aforesaid, and to aid and promote immigration.

(8.) To grant lands for terms of years or in perpetuity, and either absolutely or by way of mortgage or otherwise.

(9.) To make loans or contributions of

*Appendix*

money or money's worth for promoting any of the objects of the Company.

(10.) To acquire and hold personal property.

(11.) To acquire and hold (without licence in mortmain or other authority than this, our charter) lands in the United Kingdom, not exceeding five acres in all at any one time, for the purposes of the offices and business of the Company, and (subject to any local law) lands in any of our colonies or possessions and elsewhere convenient for carrying on the management of the affairs of the Company, and to dispose from time to time of any such lands when not required for that purpose.

(12.) To carry on any lawful commerce, trade, pursuit, business, operations or dealing whatsoever in connection with the objects of the Company.

(13.) To establish and maintain agencies in our colonies and possessions and elsewhere.

(14.) To sue and be sued by the Company's name of incorporation, as well in our courts in our United Kingdom, or in our courts in our colonies or possessions, or in our courts in foreign countries or elsewhere.

(15.) To do all lawful things incidental or conducive to the exercise or enjoyment of the rights, interests, authorities and powers of the Company in this, our charter, expressed or referred to, or any of them.

25. Within one year after the date of this, our charter, or such extended period as may be certified by our Secretary of State, there shall be executed by the members of the Company for the time being a deed of settlement, providing so far as necessary for—

(1.) The further definition of the objects and purposes of the Company.
(2.) The classes or descriptions of shares into which the capital of the Company is divided, and the calls to be made in respect thereof, and the terms and conditions of membership of the Company.
(3.) The division and distribution of profits.
(4.) General meetings of the Company; the appointment by our Secretary of State (if so required by him) of

an official director, and the number, qualification, appointment, remuneration, rotation, removal and powers of directors of the Company and of other officers of the Company.
(5.) The registration of members of the Company, and the transfer of shares in the capital of the Company.
(6.) The preparation of annual accounts to be submitted to the members at a general meeting.
(7.) The audit of those accounts by independent auditors.
(8.) The making of bye-laws.
(9.) The making and using of official seals of the Company.
(10.) The constitution and regulation of committees or local boards of management.
(11.) The making and execution of supplementary deeds of settlement.
(12.) The winding up (in case of need) of the Company's affairs.
(13.) The government and regulation of the Company and of its affairs.
(14.) Any other matters usual or proper to be provided for in respect of a chartered company.

26. The deed of settlement shall, before the execution thereof, be submitted to and approved by the Lords of our Council, and a certificate of their approval thereof, signed by the Clerk of our Council, shall be endorsed on this, our charter, and be conclusive evidence of such approval, and on the deed of settlement, and such deed of settlement shall take effect from the date of such approval, and shall be binding upon the Company, its members, officers and servants, and for all other purposes whatsoever.

27. The provisions of the deed of settlement, or of any supplementary deed for the time being in force, may be from time to time repealed, varied or added to by a supplementary deed, made and executed in such manner as the deed of settlement prescribes: Provided that the provisions of any such deed relative to the official director shall not be repealed, varied or added to without the express approval of our Secretary of State.

28. The members of the Company shall be individually liable for the debts, contracts, engagements and liabilities of the Company to the extent only of the amount, if any, for the time being unpaid on the shares held by them respectively.

29. Until such deed of settlement as aforesaid takes effect, the said James, Duke of Abercorn shall be the President; the said Alexander William George, Duke of Fife, shall be Vice-President; and the said Edric Frederick, Lord Gifford; Cecil John Rhodes; Alfred Beit; Albert Henry George Grey; and George Cawston shall be the directors of the Company; and may, on behalf of the Company, do all things necessary or proper to be done under this, our charter, by or on behalf of the Company: Provided always that, notwithstanding anything contained in the deed of settlement of the Company, the said James, Duke of Abercorn; Alexander William George, Duke of Fife; and Albert Henry George Grey shall not be subject to retire from office in accordance with its provisions, but shall be and remain directors of the Company until death, incapacity to act, or resignation, as the case may be.

30. And we do further will, ordain and declare that this, our charter, shall be acknowledged by our governors and our naval and military officers and our consuls, and our other officers in our colonies and possessions, and on the high seas and elsewhere, and they

shall severally give full force and effect to this, our charter, and shall recognise and be in all things aiding to the Company and its officers.

31. And we do further will, ordain and declare that this, our charter, shall be taken, construed and adjudged in the most favourable and beneficial sense for, and to the best advantage of the Company, as well in our courts in our United Kingdom, and in our courts in our colonies or possessions, and in our courts in foreign countries or elsewhere, notwithstanding that there may appear to be in this, our charter, any non-recital, mis-recital, uncertainty or imperfection.

32. And we do further will, ordain and declare that this, our charter, shall subsist and continue valid, notwithstanding any lawful change in the name of the Company, or in the deed of settlement thereof, such change being made with the previous approval of our Secretary of State signified under his hand.

33. And we do further will, ordain and declare that it shall be lawful for us, our heirs and successors, and we do hereby expressly reserve to ourselves, our heirs and

successors, the right and power by writing under the great seal of the United Kingdom, at the end of twenty-five years from the date of this, our charter, and at the end of every succeeding period of ten years, to add, to alter or repeal any of the provisions of this, our charter, or to enact other provisions in substitution for or in addition to any of its existing provisions: Provided that the right and power thus reserved shall be exercised only in relation to so much of this, our charter, as relates to administrative and public matters. And we do further expressly reserve to ourselves, our heirs and successors, the right to take over any buildings or works belonging to the Company and used exclusively or mainly for administrative or public purposes, on payment to the Company of such reasonable compensation as may be agreed, or as, failing agreement, may be settled by the Commissioners of our Treasury. And we do further appoint, direct and declare that any such writing under the said great seal shall have full effect and be binding upon the Company, its members, officers and servants and all other persons, and shall be of the same force, effect and validity as if its provisions had been part of and contained in these presents.

34. Provided always, and we do further declare that nothing in this, our charter, shall be deemed or taken in anywise to limit or restrict the exercise of any of our rights or powers with reference to the protection of any territories, or with reference to the government thereof, should we see fit to include the same within our dominions.

35. And we do lastly will, ordain and declare, without prejudice to any power, to repeal this, our charter, by law belonging to us, our heirs and successors, or to any of our courts, ministers or officers, independently of this present declaration and reservation, that in case at any time it is made to appear to us in our Council that the Company has substantially failed to observe and conform to the provisions of this, our charter, or that the Company is not exercising its powers under the concessions, agreements, grants and treaties aforesaid, so as to advance the interests which the Petitioners have represented to us to be likely to be advanced by the grant of this, our charter, it shall be lawful for us, our heirs and successors, and we do hereby expressly reserve and take to ourselves, our heirs and successors, the right and power by writing under the great seal of our

United Kingdom to revoke this, our charter, and to revoke and annul the privileges, powers and rights hereby granted to the Company.

In witness whereof we have caused these, our letters, to be made patent.

Witness ourself at Westminster, the twenty-ninth day of October in the fifty-third year of our reign.

By warrant under the Queen's Sign Manual.

(L.S.)  MUIR MACKENZIE.

---

ORDER IN COUNCIL of 9th May 1891.

*At the Court at Windsor, the 9th day of May 1891—*

Present,—

THE QUEEN'S MOST EXCELLENT MAJESTY.
LORD PRESIDENT.
LORD STEWARD.
EARL OF COVENTRY.

WHEREAS the territories of South Africa

situate within the limits of this order, as hereinafter described, are under the protection of Her Majesty the Queen:

And whereas by treaty, grant, usage, sufferance and other lawful means Her Majesty has power and jurisdiction in the said territories:

Now therefore Her Majesty, by virtue and in exercise of the powers by the Foreign Jurisdiction Act, 1890, or otherwise in Her Majesty vested, is pleased by and with the advice of Her Privy Council to order, and it is hereby ordered, as follows:—

I. The limits of this order are:—the parts of South Africa bounded by British Bechuanaland, the German Protectorate, the Rivers Chobe and Zambesi, the Portuguese Possessions, and the South African Republic.

II. The High Commissioner may, on Her Majesty's behalf, exercise all powers and jurisdiction which Her Majesty, at any time before or after the date of this order, had or may have within the limits of this order, and to that end may take, or cause to be taken, all such measures, and may do, or cause to be done, all such matters and things within the limits of this order as are lawful, and as in the interest of Her Majesty's service he may think expedient, subject to such instructions as he may from time to time receive from Her Majesty or through a Secretary of State.

III. The High Commissioner may appoint so many fit persons as in the interest of Her Majesty's service he may think necessary to be deputy commissioners, or resident commissioners, or assistant commissioners, or judges, magistrates, or other officers, and may define from time to time the districts within which such officers shall respectively discharge their functions.

Every such officer may exercise such powers and authorities as the High Commissioner may assign to him, subject, nevertheless, to such directions and instructions as the High Commissioner may from time to time think fit to give him. The appointment of such officers shall not abridge, alter or affect the right of the High Commissioner to execute and discharge all the powers and authorities hereby conferred upon him.

The High Commissioner may remove any officer so appointed.

IV. In the exercise of the powers and authorities hereby conferred upon him, the High Commissioner may, amongst other things, from time to time by proclamation provide for the administration of justice, the raising of revenue, and generally for the peace, order and good government of all persons within the limits of this order, including the prohibition and punishment of acts tending to disturb the public peace.

The High Commissioner, in issuing such proclamations, shall respect any native laws or customs by which the civil relations of any native chiefs, tribes or populations under Her Majesty's protection are now regulated, except so far as the same may be incompatible with the due exercise of Her Majesty's power and jurisdiction.

V. Every proclamation of the High Commissioner shall be published in the Gazette, and shall, from and after the expiration of one month from the commencement of such publication, and thereafter, until disallowed by Her Majesty, or repealed or modified by any subsequent proclamation, have effect, as if contained in this order.

VI. Her Majesty may disallow any such proclamation wholly or in part, and may signify such disallowance through a Secretary of State, and upon such disallowance being publicly notified by the High Commissioner in the Gazette the provisions so disallowed shall, one month after such publication, cease to have effect, but without prejudice to anything theretofore lawfully done thereunder.

VII. The courts of British Bechuanaland shall have in respect of matters occurring within the limits of this order the same jurisdiction, civil and criminal, original and appellate, as they respectively possess from time to time in respect of matters occurring within British Bechuanaland, and the judgments, decrees, orders and sentences of any such court made or given in the exercise of the jurisdiction hereby conferred may be enforced and executed, and appeals therefrom may be had and prosecuted in the same way as if the judgment, decree, order or sentence had been made or given under the ordinary jurisdiction of the court.

But the jurisdiction hereby conferred shall only be exercised by such courts, and in such manner and to such extent, as the Governor of British Bechuanaland shall by proclamation from time to time direct.

VIII. Subject to any proclamation made under this order, any jurisdiction exerciseable otherwise than under this order, whether by virtue of any statute or order in Council, or of any treaty, or otherwise, and whether exciseable by Her Majesty, or by any person on her behalf, or by any colonial or other court, or under any commission, or under any charter granted by Her Majesty, shall remain in full force.

IX. Judicial notice shall be taken of this order, and of the commencement thereof, and of any proclamation made under this order, and published in the Gazette, and of any treaties affecting the territories within the limits of this order, and published in the Gazette, or contained in papers presented to both Houses of Parliament, by command of Her Majesty.

X. This order shall be published in the Gazette, and shall thereupon commence and come into operation; and the High Commissioner shall give directions for the publication of this order at such places, and in such manner, and for such time or times as he thinks proper for giving due publicity thereto within the limits of this order.

XI. The orders in Council of the 27th day of

January 1885, for the establishment of civil and criminal jurisdiction in Bechuanaland, and of the 30th day of June 1890, providing for the exercise of Her Majesty's jurisdiction in certain territories in South Africa, shall continue in force until the commencement of this order and be thereupon revoked, but without prejudice to anything lawfully done thereunder, and any proclamation theretofore issued under the said orders shall continue in operation until repealed or altered by any proclamation of the High Commissioner under this order.

XII. Her Majesty may from time to time revoke, alter, add to, or amend this order.

XIII. In this order, unless the subject or context otherwise requires,—

'Her Majesty' includes Her Majesty's heirs and successors.

'Secretary of State' means one of Her Majesty's principal Secretaries of State.

'High Commissioner' means Her Majesty's High Commissioner for the time being for South Africa.

'Treaty' includes any existing or future treaty, convention or agreement between Her Majesty and any civilised power, or any native tribe, people, chief or king, and any regulation appended to any such treaty, convention or agreement.

'Gazette' means any official Gazette published by authority of the High Commissioner, and until such Gazette is instituted, means the Cape of Good Hope Government Gazette.

C. L. PEEL.

# APPENDIX (B).

AN AGREEMENT BETWEEN HER MAJESTY'S GOVERNMENT AND THE BRITISH SOUTH AFRICA COMPANY RELATIVE TO MATABELELAND AND MASHONALAND.

Clause 1. The territories referred to in this memorandum are those parts of South Africa bounded by British Bechuanaland, the German Protectorate, the Rivers Chobe and Zambesi, the Portuguese Possessions, and the South African Republic, within which the British South Africa Company, in this memorandum referred to as 'the Company,' carries on operations under and by virtue of Her Majesty's charter of October 29th, 1889; save and except the territories defined in the third section of the proclamation of the High Commissioner of September 27th, 1892, and known as the Bechuanaland Protectorate.

Clause 2. The administration of the Government of the said territories shall be conducted by the Company in accordance with its charter, and under an Administrator and a Council of four members composed of a Judge and three other members. Any two members shall form a quorum.

Clause 3. The Administrator shall be appointed by the Company, with the approval of the Secretary of State, and may be removed either by the Secretary of State or by the Company, with the approval of the Secretary of State. He shall, unless sooner removed, hold his office for a term of three years, and after the end of that term shall continue to hold his office until his successor is appointed. An Administrator whose term of office has expired may be re-appointed. The Company may appoint an Acting Administrator, of whom the Secretary of State approves, to act as Administrator during the absence on leave or incapacitating illness of the Administrator. When there is no Administrator or Acting Administrator present in the said territories and capable of acting, the duties and powers of the Administrator shall devolve on the Judge.

Clause 4. The Judge shall be appointed by the Company, with the approval of the Secretary of State, and may be removed only by the Secretary of State. He shall be a member of the Council *ex officio*.

Clause 5. The members of the Council, other than the Judge, shall be appointed by the Company, with the approval of the Secretary of State, and may be removed by the Company. On the expiration of two years from the first appointment of members, and on the expiration of every succeeding period of two years, one member of the Council shall retire from office. The first two members to retire shall be determined by agreement, or, in default of agreement, by lot. Subsequently, the member shall retire who shall have been longest in office without re-appointment. A retiring member may be re-appointed, and shall hold his office until the appointment of his successor.

Clause 6. When the Administrator or the Judge or other member of the Council resigns, is removed, or dies, the Company shall, within nine months of his resignation, removal or death, appoint a successor of whom the Secretary of State approves, and if they fail to do so the appointment may be made by the Secretary of State. A member of the Council (other than the Judge) appointed under this clause shall hold office so long only as the person in whose stead he is appointed would have been entitled to hold office.

Clause 7. The salaries of the Administrator and of the Judge shall be paid by the Company; the salaries shall be fixed by the Company, with the approval of the Secretary of State, and shall not be increased or diminished save with his approval.

Clause 8. The Administrator shall, as representative of the Company, administer the government of the said territories, but shall take the advice of his Council on all questions of importance affecting the government of the said territories. If in cases of emergency it shall be impracticable to assemble a quorum, the Administrator may take action alone, but he shall report such action to the Council at its next meeting.

Clause 9. If the Administrator dissent from the opinion of the Council, or the majority of the Council, he may overrule their opinion; but in such case he shall report the matter forthwith to the Company, with the reasons for his action, and in every such case any member of the Council who dissents may require that the reasons for his dissent shall be recorded and transmitted to the Company. The Company may rescind the decision of the Administrator, whether made with, or without, or against, the advice of the Council.

Clause 10. It shall be lawful for the Administrator, with the concurrence of at least two members of the Council, and with the approval of the High Commissioner, to frame and issue regulations; and every such regulation, after it has received the approval of the High Commissioner, shall, on its promulgation, have the force of law: Provided that either the Secretary of State or the Company may veto any such regulation at any time within twelve months of the date of approval by the High Commissioner. In case of the exercise of such veto, the regulation shall be of no force and effect, save as to any act done, right acquired, or liability incurred thereunder before the exercise of the said veto has been communicated to the Administrator and public notice of the same has been given by him.

Clause 11. A regulation approved and promulgated as aforesaid may suspend any provision of any ordinance of the Company which shall be specified therein, but every such regulation shall itself be subject to repeal or amendment by ordinance of the Company.

Clause 12. Neither the Company nor the Administrator in Council can by ordinance, or regulation, or otherwise, amend or repeal any order made by Her Majesty in Council, nor, except with the previous consent of the High Commissioner, any proclamation issued by such High Commissioner under the authority of an order made by Her Majesty in Council.

Where an ordinance of the Company, or regulation of the Administrator in Council, is in any respect repugnant to the provisions of an order made by Her Majesty in Council, or, except in the case of previous consent above specified, of a proclamation issued by the High Commissioner under such an order, it shall be read subject to such order or proclamation, and shall, to the extent of such repugnancy, but not otherwise, be and remain absolutely void and inoperative.

Clause 13. The power of making ordinances, granted to the Company under Clause 10 of its charter, shall be deemed to include the power of imposing by such ordinances all such taxes as may be necessary for the order and good government of the said territories, and for the raising of revenue therein, and also the right to impose and to collect customs duties.

Clause 14. The Company may by ordinance empower, or the Administrator in Council may by regulation empower, any local municipal body or other local authority to levy municipal rates and taxes, and to prescribe and enforce moderate money penalties for breach of local regulations.

Clause 15. The Judge shall have jurisdiction over all causes, both civil and criminal, and shall hold courts at such places as may be from time to time prescribed by proclamation of the High Commissioner or by ordinance of the Company. The procedure, rules and regulations of the said courts shall be the same, as far as is applicable, as the procedure, rules and regulations of the Supreme Court of the Cape Colony. If and when the Parliament of the Cape Colony shall express its assent thereto, Her Majesty's Government will advise the issue of an order in Council under the Foreign Jurisdiction Act, 1890, providing that appeals from the decision of the Judge shall lie to the said Supreme Court.

Clause 16. The said territories shall be

divided by the Company into magisterial districts. There shall be an appeal in all civil and criminal cases from the decision of the magistrate of any district to the Judge upon the same terms and conditions, and subject to the limitations, rules and regulations, as far as possible, which regulate appeals in the Cape Colony; and all criminal cases that would, if the same had been tried by a resident magistrate in the said colony, be liable to review by a judge of the Supreme Court shall be liable to review by the Judge.

Clause 17. All civil and criminal cases, whether between native and native, or between native and non-native, or between non-native and non-native, shall be cognisable by the courts of the Judge and magistrates within the respective jurisdictions assigned to such courts.

Clause 18. In civil cases between native and native the said courts shall decide the said cases in accordance with native law, in so far as the said law is not repugnant to principles of morality, or to any law or ordinance in force in the said territories; provided that in any suit in which the effect or consequence of any marriage contracted according to native law or custom shall be involved, any such marriage contracted by a native in the lifetime of one or more other wives of the said native, married to him according to the said law or custom, may be recognised and regarded as in all civil respects and for all civil purposes a valid marriage, in so far as such polygamous marriages are recognised by the said native law or custom. In all civil cases between natives, any magistrate or the Judge may call to his assistance two native assessors to advise him upon native law and customs, but the decision of the case shall be vested in the magistrate or Judge alone. Subject as aforesaid, the same procedure shall, as far as possible, be observed as though the said cases had been tried in the Cape Colony.

Clause 19. All criminal cases, whether between native and native, or between native and non-native, or between non-native and non-native, shall be dealt with in accordance with the laws applicable to non-natives, and the same procedure, as far as possible, shall be observed as though the said cases had been tried in the Cape Colony.

Clause 20. The magistrates shall be appointed by the Company, with the approval of the High Commissioner, and shall thereupon enter on office, but the appointments shall be subject to confirmation by the Secretary of State. The magistrates may be removed either by the Secretary of State, or by the Company with the approval of the Secretary of State.

Clause 21. The High Commissioner may suspend the Judge or any magistrate from office for misconduct, but shall immediately report to the Secretary of State the grounds of such suspension. The Secretary of State may either confirm or disallow the suspension.

Clause 22. Fines levied upon native chiefs or tribes for misconduct or rebellion may only be imposed by the Administrator in Council, and every such case shall be forthwith reported to the High Commissioner.

Clause 23. Natives shall not be subjected to any exceptional legislation save as regards liquor, arms and ammunition, and as regards the title to and occupation of land as hereinafter referred to in Clause 27, and as regards any other matter which the Administrator in Council may, with the approval of the High Commissioner and the assent of the Secretary of State, subsequently by regulation define; provided that nothing herein contained shall prevent a hut tax being imposed by legislative authority in respect of the occupation of huts by natives.

Clause 24. A commission shall be appointed to deal with all questions as to native settlements in the portion of the said territories termed Matabeleland. It shall be called the 'Land Commission,' and shall be composed of three persons, namely, the Judge, one member appointed by the Secretary of State, and one member appointed by the Company.

Clause 25. Any decision of the Land Commission shall, on sufficient cause being shown to the satisfaction of the Secretary of State, be subject to revision by him, if within twelve months from the date of the award being received by him he shall give notice of his intention to proceed to such revision.

Clause 26. The Land Commission shall continue for such time as may be approved by the Secretary of State after consultation with the Company; after which time all the powers and duties of the said Commission shall become and be vested in the Judge alone.

Clause 27. The Land Commission shall, as regards the portion of the said territories termed Matebeleland, assign to the natives now inhabiting the said portion land sufficient and suitable for their agricultural and grazing requirements, and cattle sufficient for their needs.

Clause 28. The Company shall retain the mineral rights in, over or under all land so assigned to natives; and, if the Company should require any such land for the purpose of mineral development, it shall be lawful for the Company to make application to the Land Commission, and upon good and sufficient cause shown, the Commission may order the land so required, or any portion thereof, to be given up, and assign to the natives concerned just compensation in land elsewhere, situate in as convenient a position as possible, and, as far as possible, of equal suitability for their requirements in other respects.

Clause 29. In like manner, should any land assigned to natives be required for sites for townships, railways, or for any public works, then upon application to the Land Commission, and upon good and sufficient cause being shown that the land is required for any of the above purposes, the Commission may order the land so required, or any portion thereof, to be given up, and assign to the natives concerned just compensation in land elsewhere situate in as convenient a position as possible, and, as far as

## Appendix

possible, of equal suitability for their requirements in other respects.

Clause 30. No removal of natives from any kraal, or from any portion of land assigned by the Land Commission, shall take place to another locality, except after due inquiry made upon the spot and with the authority of the said Commission.

Clause 31. The land to be assigned to natives shall include a fair and equitable portion of springs or permanent water, and of grazing and arable land.

Clause 32. The Land Commission shall have power to appoint a subordinate court, to be called the 'district land court,' in each magisterial district, consisting of the magistrate of the district, and two assessors to be appointed by the Land Commission. The said district land courts shall report or make recommendations to the Land Commission on all questions which shall be remitted to them by the Land Commission. The Land Commission may confirm or disallow, with or without amendments, any recommendations of such district land courts.

Clause 33. Natives shall have the right to

acquire and hold and dispose of landed property in the same manner as persons who are not natives, and in all respects such property shall be liable in the usual manner for any obligations for which such natives may be liable. But these provisions shall not apply to land assigned under Clause 27; and no contract for alienating or encumbering a native's land shall be valid unless it is made before a magistrate and attested by him, after satisfying himself that the native understands the bargain.

Clause 34. Persons who may be appointed to such offices as may be designated in the proclamation or proclamations by the High Commissioner, shall not (except in the case of an acting appointment) have any interest, either direct or indirect, in the commercial undertakings or shares of the Company. The offices to be designated in the said proclamations shall be such as may be agreed upon by the Secretary of State after consultation with the Company.

Clause 35. The armed forces of the Company shall not, without the permission of Her Majesty's Government, act outside the limits defined in Clause 1 of this memorandum.

Clause 36. The cost of any inquiry which the Secretary of State may think it necessary to institute into the administrative or judicial system established in the said territories shall be borne by the Company. The Company shall likewise provide such payment as may be agreed upon between Her Majesty's Govern- and the Company to the member of the Land Commission appointed by the Secretary of State.

Clause 37. None of the provisions in this memorandum contained shall be construed so as in any way to diminish or detract from the powers conferred upon Her Majesty's Secretary of State or High Commissioner by Her Majesty's order in Council of May 9th 1891, or by the charter incorporating the Company; but the said provisions shall be considered as subsidiary to, and in augmentation of, the powers so conferred : and nothing herein contained shall be construed so as in any way to diminish or detract from the powers granted to the Company by its charter.

Executed in London this 23d day of May A.D. 1894.

On behalf of Her Majesty's
    Government,
        HENRY B. LOCH,
          *High Commissioner*

The Common Seal of the British South Africa Company was affixed hereto, pursuant to a resolution of the Board of Directors, passed the 23d May 1894, in the presence of—

ABERCORN, } *Directors.*
FIFE,
HERBERT CANNING, *Secretary.*

---

The MARQUIS OF RIPON to Sir W. G. CAMERON.

DOWNING STREET, *May* 24, 1894.

SIR,—On the 13th of November last I communicated to Sir H. Loch, by telegraph, that portion of a speech made by Mr Buxton in the House of Commons on the 9th of November, in which the general views of Her Majesty's Government in regard to the future of Matabeleland were expressed.

In the course of his speech Mr Buxton spoke as follows :—' In considering the policy to be pursued in regard to the future of Matabeleland, the fact cannot be ignored that Matabeleland, as well as Mashonaland, are included within the region of South Africa described in the charter as "the principal field of the operations of the British South Africa Company," and that in the charter no distinction is made between Matebeleland and Mashonaland, the latter being already practically occupied and governed by the Company. Nor can the point be ignored that the mining and land concessions held by the Company are applicable to Matabeleland as well as to Mashonaland, *i.e.*, to the whole territory claimed by Lo Bengula. We must also bear in mind that the greater part of the operations now proceeding have been undertaken on the responsibility and at the expense of the Company. Moreover, the very important question of public feeling in South Africa must also be taken into consideration in dealing with the question.'

Mr Buxton went on to say, in effect, that the war was not to become a war of extermination or expulsion, the military system that existed must be broken down, but there was no intention or desire to expel the natives from the country, or to treat them except with humanity, mercy and justice, and that whatever settlement might be arrived at would include, as an essential feature, due safeguards for their protection and for their rights.

The question thus arose, in what form could the above principles best be applied? Her Majesty's Government carefully considered the whole matter; and, as I informed Sir H. Loch in the telegram already mentioned, they came to the conclusion that, under the existing circumstances, there were serious objections to the creation of a Crown colony in that region, or to placing Matabeleland under the direct administration of the High Commissioner. They determined, therefore, to avail themselves of the machinery at work in Mashonaland under the charter of the British South Africa Company and Her Majesty's order in Council of 9th May 1891, and to extend the existing system, with such modifications as might be considered necessary or desirable, to that part of the country known as Matabeleland. They considered it essential, however, with a view to securities for good government, that the powers of guidance and control vested in the Imperial Government by the provisions of the charter and under the order in Council should be exercised somewhat more fully than heretofore over the actions of the Company throughout their administrative area, especially in regard to the rights of, and protection over, the natives.

I was glad to learn, from subsequent correspondence, that these views practically coincided with those of Sir H. Loch.

In these circumstances the first step towards a settlement was obviously for Sir H. Loch to discuss the matter fully with Mr Rhodes, and to furnish me with suggestions as to the best means of attaining the objects in view.

This was done, and Her Majesty's Government, having now carefully considered the proposals of Sir H. Loch and Mr Rhodes, and having, moreover, had the advantage of conferring on the subject with the former personally, have finally decided on a scheme for the future administration of Mashonaland and Matabeleland, of which a copy is herewith enclosed.

This scheme, in which the substance of Sir H. Loch's proposals is embodied, has been agreed to by the British South Africa Company.

It is not necessary here to comment on the arrangement in detail; but I would point out that, as stated in the concluding clause, the new scheme of administration does not purport to supersede Her Majesty's order in Council of 9th May 1891, nor the British South Africa Company's charter of 29th October 1889, but should be read in connection with those instruments, as containing a development and reform of the existing scheme of administration. Repetition of provisions already contained in the instruments referred to has therefore, so far as practicable, been avoided.

Where the new arrangement appears to require some legislative sanction not now existing, such as the provision for local legislation by the Administrator in Council, early steps will be taken to this end ; and the occasion may possibly be taken to recast and consolidate the orders in Council and High Commissioner's proclamations affecting the Company's territory.—I have, etc., RIPON.

THE END

www.ingramcontent.com/pod-product-compliance
Lightning Source LLC
Chambersburg PA
CBHW030809230426
43667CB00008B/1129